T0209352

THE
GOD
of the
IMPOSSIBLE

Daring to Believe:
Harnessing God's Miracle-Working
Power in Your Own Life

WENDY LOVE

WESTBOW
P R E S S®
A DIVISION OF THOMAS NELSON
& ZONDERVAN

WestBow Press books may be ordered through booksellers or by contacting:

WestBow Press
A Division of Thomas Nelson & Zondervan
1663 Liberty Drive
Bloomington, IN 47403
www.westbowpress.com
844-714-3454

ISBN: 979-8-3850-0701-1 (sc)
ISBN: 979-8-3850-0699-1 (hc)
ISBN: 979-8-3850-0700-4 (e)

Library of Congress Control Number: 2023917338

Print information available on the last page.

WestBow Press rev. date: 01/09/2024

CONTENTS

INTRODUCTION

For nothing will be impossible with God. (Luke 1:37 CSB)

Are you facing an impossible situation? Have you explored all the potential options but can't see a way forward? Are you burdened by feelings of depression or anxiety due to your circumstances?

I have great news. God specializes in doing the impossible.

The Bible is full of stories of God performing miraculous feats. I can personally testify that Jesus can help us to overcome debt, addictions, unemployment, and mental health issues. He has the power to restore marriages teetering on the brink of divorce, and he gives us 'peace that passes understanding' right in the middle of life's storms.

How do you access God's miracle–working power in your own life? Through faith.

What is faith?

Now faith is confidence in what we hope for and assurance about what we do not see. (Hebrews 11:1 NIV)

Confidence: means to feel certain that something we hope for will happen.

Hope: means having a desire for a particular thing to happen.

Assurance: means having a promise that something will happen, leaving no room for doubt.

Consider the kind of faith it took for David to slay the giant Goliath. Contemplate the faith required for Gideon and his mere three hundred men to triumph over an army so vast it could not be counted. Ponder the faith exhibited by Moses in leading the Israelites out of Egypt.

Yet these individuals were ordinary people, much like you and me. Were they perfect? No, but they had a perfect heart toward God. Instead of fixating on the giants in their lives they kept their eyes on their giant, miracle–working God.

All that God asks is that we believe him.

When God promised Abram that he would have a son in his old age, despite it being physically impossible, the Bible says, "Abram believed the Lord, and he credited it to him as righteousness." (Genesis 15:6 NIV)

In Mark 9 we encounter a father who brings his son to Jesus for healing. The father implores Jesus:

> "If you can do anything, take pity on us and help us." "If you can?" said Jesus. "Everything is possible for one who believes." Immediately the boy's father exclaimed, "I do believe; help me overcome my unbelief!" (Mark 9:22–24 NIV)

Many of us can likely relate to this father. None of us possesses unwavering faith all of the time. Most of us struggle with doubt and unbelief sometimes. Yet for those who choose to believe and choose to have faith in God, amazing miracles await.

Jesus says, "If you believe, you will receive whatever you ask for in prayer." (Matthew 21:22 NIV)

Throughout the Bible, God consistently reveals himself as a God of miracles, a God who conquers giants.

He is the God of the impossible.

This book guides you through scripture, exploring some of the most extraordinary accounts of how God operates on behalf of those who choose to believe. Through unique biblical insights, accompanied by heartfelt personal narratives, you will come to know and believe in the "God of the impossible" for your own life.

[Note: Some minor details such as names have been changed to protect the privacy of those individuals.]

Part 1

THE BATTLE IS
THE LORDS

Chapter One

DEBT-FREE AT LAST

You will not have to fight this battle. Take up your positions; stand firm and see the deliverance the Lord will give you, Judah and Jerusalem. Do not be afraid; do not be discouraged. Go out to face them tomorrow, and the Lord will be with you. (2 Chronicles 20:17 NIV)

Personal Story

It was the beginning of a new year, but it felt like our lives were falling apart. Out of the depth of my pain and despair, I cried out loud, "God, I hate you. I hate you." Something I had never said or thought in my whole life. I loved the Lord. I would never have dared to speak to God that way, but I had reached breaking point. So had my husband, Luke.

After facing so many life challenges over the past twenty-five years, we were battle weary. We were exhausted. I cried my heart out until there were no tears left. What was God doing, and where was he when we were in so much pain?

Luke had lost his job the day before Christmas. It was the last straw. Like most people, we had a mortgage to pay, and I was only working part–time. We had no savings, nothing to fall back on. How would we ever make it?

But God did an incredible miracle. Just twelve months later, God had completely turned our lives around. We were debt–free and living in a new home, and Luke was enjoying a job he had only ever dreamed about.

What made the difference? What had changed?

Faith.

Faith changes everything. We'll continue this story later in the chapter.

Bible Example

Did you know that God wants to fight your battles for you?

One of my favorite Bible stories is about King Jehoshaphat and how God fought an incredible battle for the people of Judah. The story goes like this.

> After this, the Moabites and Ammonites with some of the Meunites came to wage war against Jehoshaphat. Some people came and told Jehoshaphat; "A vast army is coming against you from Edom, from the other side of the Dead Sea." (2 Chronicles 20:1–2 NIV)

King Jehoshaphat heard that not only were three armies coming to make war with him, but they were already very close. Understandably, they were terrified. They were facing an impossible situation. How could they possibly succeed in a battle against three armies? There was no warning, so there was no time to even form a battle plan. Humanly speaking, they were out of options.

What is the first thing that Jehoshaphat did? He sought the Lord. King Jehoshaphat and all the people of Judah began to seek God with all their hearts. God was their only hope, their only possibility for survival. They met at the temple of the Lord and began to pray as they had never prayed before.

In 2 Chronicles 20:12 (NIV) Jehoshaphat prayed, "We have no power to face this vast army that is attacking us. We do not know what to do, but our eyes are on you."

Whenever you find yourself in trouble, come to God and admit that you are powerless over your situation and that you are looking to him for help.

~ Remember How God Has Led You in the Past ~

One way to increase your faith when you face trouble is to recall how God has led you in the past. Keeping a journal or prayer diary is a powerful tool for the believer.

If you have been walking with God for a while, then this will not be the first time you have faced a challenge and needed God to help you. The trouble is, we often forget how God has helped us in the past. When you keep a journal or a prayer diary, you can remind yourself of the ways God has led you in the past. This greatly increases your faith that God will help you again.

How did God respond to Jehoshaphat's prayer for help? God promised to fight the battle for them. As they stood there praying, the Spirit of God spoke through one of the priests with this encouraging promise:

> This is what the LORD says to you, "Do not be afraid or discouraged because of this vast army. For the battle is not yours, but God's. Tomorrow march down against them. They will be climbing up by the Pass

3

of Ziz, and you will find them at the end of the gorge
in the Desert of Jeruel. You will not have to fight this
battle. Take up your positions; stand firm and see
the deliverance the LORD will give you, Judah and
Jerusalem. Do not be afraid; do not be discouraged.
Go out to face them tomorrow, and the LORD will be
with you." (2 Chronicles 20:15–17 NIV)

Wow, what a promise. What encouragement. God said that they
wouldn't even have to fight the battle. He would fight the battle for
them. Jehoshaphat and the people of Judah gratefully bowed down
and worshipped the Lord. Then they began to praise him.

~ They Began to Thank and
Praise God in Advance ~

Even though nothing had changed in their physical circumstances,
they demonstrated their faith in God by thanking and praising him
in advance.

There were still three armies coming to fight them. The enemy was
still very close and coming closer by the hour. They had no hope of
fighting the enemy in their own strength, but God had promised to
fight the battle for them. They praised God by faith, trusting him to
be faithful to his promise to them.

What is the Bible's definition of faith?

Now faith is confidence in what we hope for and
assurance about what we do not see. (Hebrews
11:1 NIV)

Faith means that you hope for a particular outcome, and you are
confident that God will do it.

This is what Jehoshaphat and the people of Judah were doing. They had confidence that God would do what He had promised, even though there was no physical evidence of it yet. This is how God calls each one of us to live.

~ Continue to Praise God in Advance
as You Face the Battle ~

Jehoshaphat's army went out early the next morning to the place that God had told them the enemy would be coming from. Jehoshaphat encouraged the army, saying:

Have faith in the Lord your God and you will be upheld; have faith in his prophets and you will be successful. (2 Chronicles 20:20 NIV)

Then he chose people to go out in front of the army to sing and praise God as they marched toward the battle. Notice that the singers went in front of the soldiers. This is an important principle. Faith, belief, praise, and thanksgiving come first, then God acts.

~ God Fought the Battle for Them
Just as He Had Promised ~

Second Chronicles 20:22–24 says:

As they began to sing and praise, the Lord set ambushes against the men of Ammon and Moab and Mount Seir who were invading Judah, and they were defeated. The Ammonites and Moabites rose up against the men from Mount Seir to destroy and annihilate them. After they finished slaughtering the men from Seir, they helped to destroy one another. When the men of Judah came to the place that overlooks the desert and looked toward the vast army, they saw only dead bodies lying on the ground; no one had escaped.

When God sees our faith and hears our praise, it moves his heart to act on our behalf and to fight our battle for us.

Not only did God fight the battle for them, but he also gave them all the wealth and possessions that had belonged to the enemy. There was so much plunder that it took three days to collect it.

God is so good. Acquiring great possessions had not even been part of God's promise to them, but we serve a super–abundant God who does even more than we ask of him.

Ephesians 3:20–21 (AMP) says:

> Now to Him who is able to [carry out His purpose and] do superabundantly more than all that we dare ask or think [infinitely beyond our greatest prayers, hopes, or dreams], according to His power that is at work within us, to Him be the glory in the church and in Christ Jesus throughout all generations forever and ever. Amen.

~ God Gives Them Peace all Around Them ~

But God doesn't finish His blessing there. Second Chronicles 20:29–30 says:

> The fear of God came on all the surrounding kingdoms when they heard how the Lord had fought against the enemies of Israel. And the kingdom of Jehoshaphat was at peace, for his God had given him rest on every side.

When all the nations who lived around Judah heard how God had miraculously rescued his people, they dared not come against them. God gave his people peace from all the countries around them.

God had done three key things:

1. He fought the battle for them.
2. He gave them all the wealth and possessions of the enemy.
3. He gave them his peace.

Why did God do this? Because they sought God with all their hearts, believed His promise to them, and praised him in advance. Faith, praise, and gratitude get God's attention.

So how does this story relate to our lives today?

Continuation of Personal Story

I had always been a person of strong faith, but when Luke lost his job, it was the last straw. We had faced many hard times in the past twenty-five years. We couldn't take another setback. We both spiraled down into the deepest depression we had experienced in years.

I had forgotten how bad depression was, really bad depression. Our pain was so intense. It felt like a physical force, beating us over and over again. Down, down we went, ever deeper into depression and despair. I hit rock bottom.

I knew I couldn't physically stand to feel this bad anymore. I had to do something. I realized that a big part of the reason I was so depressed was because I had lost my faith in God. I also realized that I was allowing my negative thoughts to consume me, dragging me down even further.

Once I realized this, I did two things:

1. I made a choice to trust God even in the midst of my pain.

I made a conscious choice to trust God again even though I didn't understand what he was doing. It was hard. I didn't feel like trusting God. I really felt that he had really let us down.

2. I chose to start being thankful on purpose.

I purposefully looked for things I could be thankful for. Just simple things like "Thank you that my arms and legs work" and "Thank you for clean drinking water".

To my surprise, just by doing these two things, little by little, day by day, I started to feel better. Within a few weeks, the depression had lifted, and I had a renewed faith in God.

Don't get me wrong. I'm not saying that clinical depression can be cured just by trusting God and practicing gratitude. I have found medication to be lifesaving as I have struggled with my mental health over the years. What I am saying is that if you are going through a particularly bad depressive episode, you can improve how you feel by putting your trust in God and making a choice to be thankful for what you do have.

~ The Biblical Law of Sowing and Reaping ~

I really enjoy listening to a preacher named Jerry Savelle. One of the principles I had been learning from him was about was the biblical law of 'sowing and reaping.'

This principle works in a similar way to a farmer planting crops in his field. He sows seed and in due time, he reaps a harvest.

A man reaps what he sows. (Galatians 6:7–8 NIV)

In the biblical law of 'sowing and reaping', the type of seed you sow depends on the type of harvest you need. We needed a financial miracle, so I decided to 'sow' (give away) a certain amount of money.

I prayed and asked God to give me a hundredfold financial 'harvest' in return for my giving (meaning that I would receive one hundred times the amount I had given away). I had done this once before when we were in desperate need, and God had graciously given us the hundredfold harvest I had asked him for (see chapter 4). This experience had given me faith that God could and would do it again.

An important part of this process is to find Bible texts that support what you are believing for so that you have something to anchor your faith to. The main Bible text I chose was Genesis 26:12 (NIV):

> Isaac planted crops in that land and the same year
> reaped a hundredfold, because the Lord blessed him.

Isaac reaped this bountiful harvest during a time of famine. We were in the middle of a financial famine. I knew that I could claim this Bible text for myself because in Galatians 3:29 (NIV) it says,

> If you belong to Christ, then you are Abraham's seed,
> and heirs according to the promise.

The promises that God gave to Abraham were not just for Abraham's physical seed (his natural descendants) but for all of us who believe in Jesus Christ.

~ Becoming Debt–Free ~

We lived in an old, run–down house on a busy main road. We had lived there for eighteen years and had raised our family there. I saw our friends move into nicer houses, but I didn't think that would ever happen to us. God helped me learn to be content with our old house.

As my husband Luke used to say, "It's not much, but it's ours and it's full of love".

As we came toward the end of the year, I felt that God was prompting me to put our house up for sale. Luke agreed and we signed up with a real estate agent. On his first inspection, the agent said, "The house isn't worth much, but the land may be valuable to a developer".

It was challenging trying to sell a house during Covid restrictions. The agent could only take one person or one couple through the house at a time, each one by private appointment. This limited the number of prospective buyers who saw the property.

But that didn't stop God.

Just six weeks after putting our old house on the market, the agent rang and said he had an offer for us. We were excited, yet somewhat nervous to find out what the offer was. When the agent told us the figure, we couldn't believe our ears. It was higher than we had dared to hope that our house might be worth. We eagerly signed the contract of sale.

Just three days later, we went to have a look at a lovely new townhouse in our local area. We fell in love with it immediately. It was only three years old, very spacious, and considerably cheaper than similar townhouses that we had looked at. We put in an offer immediately. After some negotiation, we agreed on a price.

When I calculated the difference between the sale price of our old house and the purchase price of the new townhouse, it was exactly one hundred times the amount I had given away, just as God promised in his Word. This paid off our entire mortgage. We were debt-free!

It was a total miracle, something we had never dreamed would happen to us. We felt overwhelmed with gratitude to God for his goodness and faithfulness. God had literally brought Ephesians 3:20–21 (NIV) true in our lives.

> Now to him who is able to do immeasurably more than all we ask or imagine, according to the power that is at work within us, to him be glory in the church and in Christ Jesus throughout all generations, for ever and ever! Amen.

Take a moment to reflect on your own life. What battles are you facing? God wants to fight your battle for you.

Key Learnings from this Chapter

When you face trouble or hardship in your life:

1. Seek the Lord with all your heart and tell him about what you are facing.
2. Admit that you are powerless over the situation and that you don't know what to do.
3. Worship God for His majesty, greatness, and strength, confident that no situation is too hard for him to handle.
4. Recall the way God has helped you in the past. This will build up your faith that God will help you again.
5. Ask God for his help. Ask him to fight the battle for you.
6. Search the Bible for God's promises that you can hold on to while you are waiting for him to work.
7. Start praising God in advance, before you see the answer.
8. If God tells you to take some action, obey him.
9. Watch God work on your behalf.
10. Praise God for His deliverance. Enjoy the peace that God brings after fighting the battle with and for you.

Prayer

Dear Lord Jesus, thank you that when we face life's challenges, you are willing to fight the battle for us. You are so faithful. Help us to keep on believing your promises to us, no matter what our circumstances look like. Remind us to praise you and thank you in advance. In Jesus Name, Amen.

Chapter Two

THE GIANT OF ADDICTION

What is impossible with man is possible with God.
(Luke 18:27 NIV)

Personal Story

There was a loud explosion, followed by the sound of shattering glass. Luke collapsed to the ground, crying out in pain.

Luke had been inspecting the paint job on his car. The automotive painter quickly went over to see what had happened. One of the heating lamps had exploded near Luke's face leaving glass in his left eye.

The painter scrambled to get his car out, helped Luke get in the front seat, and drove him to the emergency department of the local hospital. The triage nurse at the hospital took one look at Luke's eye and immediately had him transferred to the Eye and Ear Hospital.

For the next six hours, the doctors and nurses worked on his eye. At 2:00 am, they decided to stop for the night and continue in the morning. The next day, they gave Luke a general anesthetic and continued their work on his eye. They were able to remove most of the glass fragments, but not all of them. Luke was in the hospital for five days and five nights. They discharged him from the hospital with two stitches on his eyeball. This was painful and uncomfortable and made it almost impossible to sleep.

~ The Spider–Web of Addiction~

Six weeks later, Luke went to a party with his brother. It was the first time that he had ever gotten drunk. Normally he hated alcohol. He couldn't stand the taste or the smell of it. When he went out with friends, he was always the 'designated driver' because he never drank. But that night, everything changed.

After getting home from the party, Luke slept soundly through the night for the first time since the accident. He was so relieved to be able to sleep that he decided to drink a lot the next night, and the next night after that. He had finally found something that worked! Every night he drank himself to sleep, not realizing that he was quickly getting caught in the spider–web of addiction.

Like people becoming addicted to pain relief medication or sleeping medication, it starts out innocently enough, as a solution to a problem. Unfortunately, what initially appears to be the 'solution' becomes a whole new 'problem'.

We had been married for two years before Luke confessed to me how much he drank every night. He had managed to hide it from me all that time.

Thirty years later, Luke was still trapped in the 'giant' of alcohol addiction until one day God miraculously intervened. We will read about this miracle later in the chapter.

~ God Will Fight our Giants for Us ~

Are you facing giants in your life today? What kind of giants are you facing? Financial giants? Health giants? Relationship giants? Work giants? Depression giants? As long as we live in this sinful world, we will face giants of various kinds, but take heart, God is bigger than any giants you are facing.

Bible Example

In this chapter, we read the story of David and Goliath. Just as God gave David the victory over Goliath, so God gave Luke the victory over his alcohol addiction.

~ David is Anointed King ~

To help us better understand the story of David and Goliath, it is useful to go back and read about when David is first anointed as the next king.

God had told the prophet Samuel that he had chosen one of the sons of Jesse to be the next king. God directed Samuel to have each of Jesse's sons walk in front of him. God would tell him which one would be king. They were all strong and handsome, but none of them was the one God had chosen.

> But the Lord said to Samuel, "Do not consider his appearance or his height, for I have rejected him. The Lord does not look at the things people look at. People look at the outward appearance, but the Lord looks at the heart." (1 Samuel 16:7 NIV)

This is encouraging for us all. God is not interested in our looks, our education, or our experience. God only looks at our hearts. He is looking for people who will seek him, rely on him, and believe in him.

David was the youngest son, and he was out in the hills looking after the family's sheep. David's father and brothers thought so little of him that they hadn't even bothered to bring him in to present him to Samuel. When God rejected each one of Jesse's sons, Samuel asked Jesse if he had any other sons. "'There is still the youngest", Jesse answered. 'He is tending the sheep.'" (1 Samuel 16:11 NIV) Samuel told him to go and bring the youngest son to him.

When David passed in front of Samuel, God told Samuel that David was the one He had chosen to be the next king. God knew David's heart. He had the heart of faith that God was looking for.

~ God Begins Training to be King ~

> From that day on the Spirit of the Lord came powerfully upon David. (1 Samuel 16:13 NIV)

God filled David with his Spirit. God started to prepare David to be king, right where he was, out minding the sheep. David had no one else to talk to out there except God himself. He wrote hundreds of songs of praise to God. God also taught him to be a brave warrior, fighting and killing lions and bears that came to attack the sheep.

Then God arranged for David to become a personal musician for King Saul. Although Saul would have regarded him as just another servant, this experience gave David a firsthand education about what it means to be king and about how a palace is run.

~ You are in the Right Place at the Right Time ~

God positions each one of us in the right place at the right time. So take heart. If God has put a dream in your heart to do something special for him and it feels like nothing is happening, you can be confident that God is at work behind the scenes, putting everything in place. Stay faithful. Keep believing. You are in God's perfect timing and his perfect will for your life.

~ Israel at War with the Philistines ~

Israel and the Philistines were at war. The Philistines controlled one hill, and the Israelites controlled another. The valley was between them. The Philistines had a champion fighter named Goliath. He was about nine feet four inches tall. Every day, Goliath came out to challenge the army of Israel to send a man to fight him. Every time Goliath came out to challenge the Israelites to fight, they ran away in fear. They were terrified of him.

David's three eldest brothers had gone to fight the war. David's father asked him to go and check how his brothers were and how the war was going. Just as David got there, the giant, Goliath came out and shouted his usual defiant taunt to the Israelites, and once again, the army of Israel ran away in fear.

> David asked the men standing near him, "What will be done for the man who kills this Philistine and removes this disgrace from Israel? Who is this uncircumcised Philistine that he should defy the armies of the living God?" (1 Samuel 17:26 NIV)

Instead of looking at the giant size of Goliath, David was looking at the giant God that he served. Out of the entire Israelite army, David was the only one who believed in God's miracle–working power to do the impossible.

~ David Fights Goliath ~

> What David said was overheard and reported to Saul, and Saul sent for him. David said to Saul, "Let no one lose heart on account of this Philistine; your servant will go and fight him." (1 Samuel 17:31–32 NIV)

When Saul expressed doubt that David had the battle experience required to fight Goliath, David told Saul that while he had been out watching the sheep, he had fought and killed both lions and bears to protect the sheep. Saul reluctantly agreed to let David go and fight Goliath. He insisted on giving David his own armor to wear, but it was too big for David and he was not used to it, so he took it off. David simply went to the brook, selected five smooth stones, and had his sling ready.

As David came closer to Goliath, Goliath looked at him and cursed him by his gods. David wasn't looking at Goliath's height, weight, strength, experience, or armor, He was looking to his giant God.

> David said to the Philistine, "You come against me with sword and spear and javelin, but I come against you in the name of the Lord Almighty, the God of the armies of Israel, whom you have defied. This day the Lord will deliver you into my hands, and I'll strike you down and cut off your head. This very day I will give the carcasses of the Philistine army to the birds and the wild animals, and the whole world will know that there is a God in Israel. All those gathered here will know that it is not by sword or spear that the Lord saves; for the battle is the Lord's, and he will give all of you into our hands."

> As the Philistine moved closer to attack him, David ran quickly toward the battle line to meet him. Reaching into his bag and taking out a stone, he slung it and struck the Philistine on the forehead. The stone sank into his forehead, and he fell face down on the ground. (1 Samuel 17:45–49 NIV)

When the Philistines saw that their champion was dead, they ran for their lives. The army of Israel charged after them.

While it might sound hard to believe that David would get the right shot the first time, you need to remember two things:

1. David was looking to God for victory. He was not looking at his own strength, skill, or experience.
2. David had been out in the hills for years, with nothing to do except take care of the sheep and practice with his sling. In David's well–trained hands, the sling was a deadly accurate weapon. He aimed straight at Goliath's uncovered forehead and hit him dead center.

What giants are you facing in your life today? No matter how big or scary your giants look, none of them are bigger than our giant God. Choose to be like David. Choose faith in God over fear of your circumstances. The God who specializes in doing the impossible will fight your battle with and for you.

Continuation of Personal Story

Luke continued to drink every day for thirty years. In the daytime, he was his normal self, the wonderful man I loved, but at night he would drink himself to sleep.

Like most addicts, the addictive substance was just a form of "self–medicating" another problem. It could be to disguise depression or some other mental or emotional pain. It may be to help with physical pain. It may be to help with sleep. Although it was hard to see him like this every night, it soon became part of our 'normal' life.

Luke finally started to realize that alcohol had become a serious problem. He started going to various doctors to try to get help. Unfortunately, the doctors were no help at all. One of them asked him "Would you rob a bank to get alcohol?" Luke said, "Of course not." So, the doctor told him he was fine, just try to cut back on the grog a bit. After trying doctor after doctor, without finding anyone who would help him, Luke gave up trying. These were the darkest days of all. He drank more and more and more. I prayed and prayed for Luke to stop drinking, but after thirty years, I didn't think it was very likely that he would stop.

~ Things Start to Improve ~

Luke's brother gave me a teaching from Jerry Savelle called "The Hand of God". It changed my life.

One of the Bible stories in the teaching was from Luke 18. I won't go into the story here, but at the end of the story in Luke 18:7–8 (NIV) it says:

> And will not God bring about justice for his chosen ones, who cry out to him day and night? Will he keep putting them off? I tell you, he will see that they get justice, and quickly. However, when the Son of Man comes, will he find faith on the earth?

Jerry Savelle encouraged us to bring this story before God and claim it for ourselves, asking God to "avenge us of our adversary." The "adversary" spoken of here, is the devil, who spends all his time trying to destroy our lives.

When I began claiming these Bible texts with God, I started to see Luke slowly change. He didn't stop drinking immediately, but he generally became calmer and happier. I could see him slowly changing before my eyes and I praised God for it.

~ Victory Over the Giant of Addiction ~

Luke tried to stop drinking many times, including going to rehab twice, but without long–term success. After thirty years of drinking, his liver was struggling to function.

One day, Luke became violently ill for about five days. He was too sick to even drink alcohol. He attributed the sickness to his drinking, and he finally decided enough was enough. It was time to stop. Miraculously, with God's help, he made it through each day without drinking and finally stopped drinking for good. It has now been seven years since Luke stopped drinking and he hasn't touched a drop of alcohol since.

He is now back to the wonderful man I first married. After thirty–two years of marriage, we still love, laugh, and truly enjoy each other's company. It's an absolute miracle. Praise God, who fights the giants in our lives.

Key Learnings from this Chapter

1. We all face various giants, but God can overcome any giant in our life.
2. When you face a giant in your life, take no notice of how big or scary it looks. Keep your eyes on our giant God.
3. Out of the entire army of Israel, David was the only person who believed in the miracle–working power of God. Every other person in the entire Israelite army was living in unbelief. Don't be an unbelieving believer.
4. If you believe that God has put a dream in your heart and it looks like nothing is happening, take heart. You are in the right place at the right time. God is working behind the scenes. God is training you for your final destiny, right where you are.
5. No matter how long your battle has been going on, don't give up hope. God can deliver you.

Prayer

Dear Lord, you know that today I am facing the giant of _____ (fill in the blank). Lord, I cannot do this alone.

I need you desperately. I look to you, trusting in you to fight this battle for me. I believe in you, dear Lord. I know that you are far bigger than any earthly giant I will ever face. Thank you Lord. In Jesus' name, Amen.

Chapter Three

MIRACLE IN TWENTY-FOUR HOURS

Jesus said, "Did I not tell you that if you believe, you
will see the glory of God?" (John 11:40 NIV)

Did you know that it's possible for God to turn around an impossible
situation in just twenty–four hours? He did it in this Bible story and
He did it for us.

Personal Story

With shaky hands, I dropped the letter to the floor. It was a totally
unexpected bill for many tens of thousands of dollars. Unemployment
was high and neither of us had a job at the time. No one is going to
lend money to two people who are unemployed. What would we do?
How could we possibly pay for it? It had been nearly twenty years since
we had last bought and sold real estate, so we had forgotten all about
costs like Stamp Duty. I picked up the letter off the floor. With my
heart pounding with anxiety, I went outside to tell Luke the bad news.

Just twenty–four hours later, God had miraculously sorted it all out
for us. We did not have to pay a cent. I will cover more about God's
miraculous provision later in the chapter.

Bible Example

~ Siege and Famine in Samaria ~

In this amazing Bible story, God miraculously rescued his people in twenty–four hours.

In second Kings 6 and 7, we read that a huge enemy had come from Aram and laid siege to the city of Samaria. The siege had dragged on for months and eventually there was almost no food left in the city. People were starving. The people of Samaria were calling out to the King to help them.

> The king replied, "If the Lord does not help you, where can I get help for you?" (2 Kings 6:27 NIV)

The King went to see the prophet Elisha to seek God's guidance and help.

> Elisha replied, "Hear the word of the Lord. This is what the Lord says: About this time tomorrow, a seah of the finest flour will sell for a shekel and two seahs of barley for a shekel at the gate of Samaria." (2 Kings 7:1 NIV)

There was only a tiny amount of food left in the city and it was selling at outrageous prices. Yet here, Elisha was saying that in twenty–four hours, there would be an abundance of food and that it would be cheap! How could this possibly happen?

> The officer on whose arm the king was leaning said to the man of God, "Look, even if the Lord should open the floodgates of the heavens, could this happen?" "You will see it with your own eyes," answered Elisha, "but you will not eat any of it!" (2 Kings 7:2 NIV)

The officer did not believe that what Elisha had said was possible. Of course, it was impossible humanly speaking, but nothing is impossible for God.

~ God Sends the Enemy Running for Their Lives ~

God intervenes to save His people. Second Kings 7:6–7 (NIV) says:

> The Lord had caused the Arameans to hear the sound of chariots and horses and a great army, so that they said to one another, "Look, the king of Israel has hired the Hittite and Egyptian kings to attack us!" So they got up and fled in the dusk and abandoned their tents and their horses and donkeys. They left the camp as it was and ran for their lives.

The people of Israel had no idea what God had done and that the enemy had left everything and run away.

> Now there were four men with leprosy at the entrance of the city gate. They said to each other, "Why stay here until we die? If we say, We'll go into the city— the famine is there, and we will die. And if we stay here, we will die. So let's go over to the camp of the Arameans and surrender. If they spare us, we live; if they kill us, then we die." At dusk they got up and went to the camp of the Arameans. When they reached the edge of the camp, no one was there. (2 Kings 7:3–5 NIV)

Gingerly, they went into the first tent and peeked inside it. There was no one there. They checked the second tent and the third, then the rest of the camp. They couldn't believe their eyes. The entire army had disappeared! The enemy had left their possessions strewn along the road in their hurry to leave the camp. There was food, clothing, gold, silver, armor, horses, donkeys, everything, just there for the taking.

The men with leprosy began to eat the food hungrily. Then they started putting the clothing on and shoving handfuls of gold and silver into their pockets. They went from tent to tent, taking everything they could carry, and stuffing themselves full of food. They were jumping and dancing with joy. It was beyond belief. Then they realized that keeping this all to themselves wasn't right.

> Then they said to each other, "What we're doing is not right. This is a day of good news and we are keeping it to ourselves. If we wait until daylight, punishment will overtake us. Let's go at once and report this to the royal palace."
>
> So they went and called out to the city gatekeepers and told them, "We went into the Aramean camp and no one was there, not a sound of anyone, only tethered horses and donkeys, and the tents left just as they were." The gatekeepers shouted the news, and it was reported within the palace. (2 Kings 7:9–11 NIV)

The King was certain it was a trap set by the enemy, to lure them out of the relative safety of the city.

> The king got up in the night and said to his officers, "I will tell you what the Arameans have done to us. They know we are starving; so they have left the camp to hide in the countryside, thinking, They will surely come out, and then we will take them alive and get into the city." (2 Kings 7:12 NIV)

But since they were going to starve to death anyway, they decided to investigate for themselves.

> So they selected two chariots with their horses, and the king sent them after the Aramean army. He commanded the drivers, "Go and find out what has happened." They followed them as far as the Jordan, and they found the whole road strewn with the clothing and equipment the Arameans had thrown away in their headlong flight. So the messengers returned and reported to the king. Then the people went out and plundered the camp of the Arameans. So a seah of the finest flour sold for a shekel, and two seahs of barley sold for a shekel, as the LORD had said.
> (2 Kings 7:14–16 NIV)

But the King's servant, who had not believed Elisha when he said God would rescue them, did not get to eat any of it, just as Elisha had predicted. He was trampled to death in the city gateway as the citizens of the city poured out in the rush to get food. Not only did the people now have an abundance of food, but they had also gained all the wealth and possessions of the enemy, who had left everything behind when they had fled. They were free. God had frightened the enemy away. In twenty–four hours, they had received their miracle just as Elisha had promised.

Continuation of Personal Story

When we received the letter from the lawyer that there was a Stamp Duty bill of many tens of thousands of dollars, the shock took our breath away. Where were we supposed to find the money? Little did we know that God already had a plan in place.

We received some junk mail the following day and were about to throw it in the bin when something caught Luke's eye. It was a newsletter from the Real Estate agency. There was an article in the newsletter about Stamp Duty. It said that people with a Health Care card were exempt from Stamp Duty. We re–read it just to check if we had read it correctly. As we were unemployed at the time, Luke and I both had a Health Care Card.

We got into the car and drove straight to the lawyer's office to check if the Stamp Duty exemption applied to us. They entered all our information into their database. Sure enough, when they entered our Health Care card details into the system, it calculated our Stamp Duty charge as zero. It was unbelievable. Relief and joy washed over us. We didn't have to pay the huge Stamp Duty charge after all.

God is so good. When we had no way to pay such a huge expense, God took care of it. This reminded me of Romans 8:28 (NIV) which says:

> And we know that in all things God works for the good of those who love him, who have been called according to His purpose.

Key Learnings from this Chapter

1. God is always in control, no matter how bad our circumstances look.
2. God can turn things around very quickly. Nothing is impossible for him.
3. God delights in taking a negative situation and bringing good out of it.
4. God still does miracles today. All He asks is that we believe him.

Prayer

Dear Father God, thankyou that when we are in trouble, we can come to you and know with confidence that you will take care of us. Thank you that you take our bad situations and bring good out of them. Thank you for your faithfulness and mercy. In Jesus Name, Amen.

Chapter Four

GOD DOES A LOT
WITH A LITTLE

For nothing will be impossible with God. (Luke
1:37 CSB)

Personal Story

With a heavy heart, I checked our dwindling bank balance, bracing
myself for disappointing news. To my dismay, it was even worse than
I had expected – only sixteen dollars left. How could we possibly
provide for our family of four and cover our mortgage next month? It
seemed impossible. As I turned to God in prayer about our desperate
situation, I decided to do something radical to show God that I trusted
him to provide for our needs.

I had been listening to a teaching by Jerry Savelle about a special prayer
called 'The Prayer of Petition'. In this type of prayer, you look up Bible
promises that relate to your need and write them down. You bring these
promises before God and specify you what you need him to provide.
Then you 'sow a seed' and believe God for a miraculous harvest.

The seed you sow depends on what you need. In this case, my need was
for finances, so I took the sixteen dollars and donated it to a worthy
cause. By faith, I trusted that God would bless me with a hundredfold

return on my donation (seed sown), amounting to a harvest of $1,600. With this sum, I could cover the mortgage and purchase essential items.

Where did I find the promise of a hundredfold harvest from? In Genesis 26:12 (AMPC) the Bible says:

> Then Isaac sowed seed in that land and received in the same year a hundred times as much as he had planted, and the Lord favored him with blessings.

God had promised to bless Abraham and his seed (descendants) abundantly. According to Galatians 3:29 (NIV), since I am a believer in Jesus Christ, I am also counted as Abraham's seed and can claim the same promised blessings.

Just two days after donating the sixteen dollars, I received a surprise call from a former colleague. He offered me a part–time position starting immediately. I was astounded that he contacted me so unexpectedly, only two days after I had given the money away (sown my seed). I knew with certainty that this was God at work.

As I began working, my hours soon increased from two days to four days per week. He even put me on a higher pay rate than I had been earning previously. Within two weeks of sowing the sixteen dollars 'seed' and trusting God for a miraculous 'harvest', I received a hundredfold return of $1,600 through my wages. I gratefully praised God for his wondrous intervention.

God specializes in doing a lot with a little.

Bible Example

In this chapter, we explore the remarkable story of Gideon. God called Gideon to lead an army of merely three hundred men to overcome an army so large that it was impossible to count them. God loves partnering with ordinary, fearful, weak human beings and accomplishing extraordinary things through them.

Like the miracle with my sixteen dollars, God took a small amount and did a miracle with it.

~ A Formidable Army Threatens Israel ~

Once again, the people of Israel had stopped worshipping the one true God and started worshipping the gods of other nations, so God had permitted the formidable army of Midian to oppress them.

The Midianites would routinely raid Israel, plundering their food and possessions, leaving the Israelites with nothing. The Israelites had no choice but to leave their homes and live in caves. Eventually, driven by desperation, Israel cried out to God for deliverance.

~ The Angel of the Lord Appears to Gideon ~

One day, an Israelite named Gideon was hiding in a wine press, grinding grain, trying to keep it from the Midianites, when suddenly the angel of the Lord appeared to him. Judges 6:12–14 (ICB) records their encounter.

> The angel of the Lord appeared to Gideon and said, "The Lord is with you, mighty warrior!" Then Gideon said, "Pardon me, sir. If the Lord is with us, why are we having so many troubles? Our ancestors told us he did miracles. They told us the Lord brought them out of Egypt. But now he has left us. He has allowed the Midianites to defeat us. The Lord turned to Gideon and said, "You have the strength to save the people of Israel. Go and save them from the Midianites. I am the one who is sending you."

Gideon was astounded. He was just an ordinary man, not even a soldier. He was hiding in fear from the ruthless enemy. Yet, God looked beyond Gideon's present state and saw the person He was about to transform him into—a "mighty warrior" (Judges 6:12, ICB).

According to Romans 4:17 (ESV) God "calls into existence the things that do not exist." Frequently, God communicates with people in the Bible as if something has already happened, even though it has not occurred in reality. When God spoke to Abraham, he declared "I have made you a father of many nations" (Genesis 17:5 NIV), even though Abraham does not receive the child of promise until many years later. God commended Abraham for believing in what seemed impossible in the natural realm.

God sees the end from the beginning. He has a unique purpose for each one of us. He sees us as the person he is going to transform us into. He sees our weaknesses and makes us strong. He sees our fear and makes us courageous. He sees our lack of ability and gives us his supernatural ability. In this case, God takes an ordinary man and makes him into a warrior.

~ Gideon Starts Making Excuses ~

Gideon made excuses about why he couldn't do what God has asked of him.

There is a striking resemblance between when God called Gideon and when God called Moses (see chapter 10). Like Gideon, Moses made all kinds of excuses about why he couldn't do what God asked of him, yet God transforms Moses into one of the greatest leaders in history. Both Gideon and Moses are listed in Hebrews 11 amongst the heroes of faith, yet they both started out terrified about what God was asking them to do. They were focused on their own limited strength and ability instead of focusing on God's infinite strength and ability.

We can gain courage from this. Throughout history, God has partnered with fearful, imperfect people like you and me and accomplished extraordinary things through them.

~ The Spirit of the Lord Empowers Gideon ~

In Judges 6:34 (NIV), we read, "Then the Spirit of the Lord came on Gideon." This is the key to success. When God's Spirit enters our lives, he empowers and equips us to accomplish our God–given purpose.

Struggling to believe that God would truly use him to deliver Israel from the Midianites, Gideon asked for some miraculous signs to confirm God's words. God graciously provided Gideon with the signs he requested, which bolstered his faith. After receiving these miraculous signs, Gideon gained the confidence to rally the men of Israel and prepare to attack the enemy. Thirty–two thousand men responded to Gideon's call, ready to fight.

~ God Says There are Too Many Men ~

> Then the Lord said to Gideon, "You have too many men to defeat the Midianites. I don't want the Israelites to brag that they saved themselves. So now, announce to the people, anyone who is afraid may leave Mount Gilead. He may go back home." So 22,000 men went back home. But 10,000 remained. Then the Lord said to Gideon, "There are still too many men." Judges 7:2–4 (ICB)

God told Gideon that only three hundred men were to fight in the battle, despite the fact that they were facing an enormous army and impossible odds. God graciously gave Gideon one more sign to encourage him. After this sign, Gideon was convinced that God would deliver the enemy into their hands.

In Judges 7:15 (ICB), Gideon returned to the Israelite camp and proclaimed, "Get up! The Lord has defeated the army of Midian for you!" Notice that Gideon now spoke with unwavering faith, echoing the same confidence God had shown him—as if the battle had already been won.

~ Midian is Defeated ~

Gideon divided the three hundred men into three groups. He gave each man a trumpet and an empty jar. A burning torch was inside each jar. Gideon told the men, "Watch me and do what I do. When I get to the edge of the camp, do what I do. Surround the enemy camp. I and everyone with me will blow our trumpets. When we blow our trumpets, you blow your trumpets, too. Then shout, For the Lord and for Gideon!" (Judges 7:16–18 ICB)

When Gideon's three hundred men blew their trumpets, the Lord caused all the men of Midian to fight each other with their swords! (Judges 7:22 ICB)

God made the enemy think that they were surrounded, with no hope of escape. They turned on each other and then ran for their lives. Gideon sent messengers to the tribes of Israel, urging them to pursue the remaining enemy forces. God brings about this incredible victory, after which, he gave Israel forty years of peace.

~ God Will Fight Our Battles for Us ~

We are often afraid about the challenging situations that we face, but God will fight the battle for us. It does not depend on our own strength or abilities. He will do the fighting. All he asks is that we believe him, trust in him and give him the glory for the victory.

Continuation of Personal Story

You would think that after God had blessed me so much by miraculously turning sixteen dollars into sixteen hundred dollars, that my faith and belief would be unshakeable, but sadly, this was not the case. Once the initial relief of having a job wore off, I then started to doubt whether I had the ability to do the job. It had been fifteen years since I had done this type of work.

As human beings, we are often fickle in our faith. One moment, we stand firm with unwavering confidence that God will come through for us, and the next, we find ourselves overwhelmed by fear. During that time, I reflected in my journal, "Even though I have had such overwhelming proof that God is with me and that belief in God is all that matters, yet this week, I find myself nervous, fearful, and not trusting God to help me do the job he so miraculously gave me. Yet last week I was at complete peace and rest, knowing God was with me. I am no better than the Israelites."

Although I was truly grateful for the job God had given me, I still doubted him. Instead of relying on God's strength and ability to do the job, I was looking to my own limited strength and ability. I knew it was crucial to get my eyes back on God again. Day by day, I asked God to give me wisdom, favor, and strength to do the job.

Again, I had worried for nothing. I loved the job. Later, I wrote in my journal "The job was fine, easy and pleasant, so I was terrified for nothing. Trust God. He always has your back!"

Key Learnings from this Chapter

1. Nothing is impossible with God.
2. God delights in partnering with ordinary human beings and accomplishing extraordinary things through them.

3. God ensures that there is no doubt that the victory belongs to him, not to us.
4. God can do a lot with a little.
5. Trust God to guide and help you in every situation.

Prayer

Thank you, precious Lord Jesus that you can take an ordinary person like me and do something extraordinary through me. I want to be that person, Lord. I put my trust and faith in you completely. Jesus precious name, Amen.

Chapter Five

RESTORATION OF OUR MARRIAGE

The LORD will fight for you; you need only to be still.
(Exodus 14:14 NIV)

Personal Story

It was the last straw. My marriage had become a sea of pain and suffering and I felt like I was drowning. I felt I had no choice but to leave. I knew that my husband, Luke, was also drowning, in his alcohol addiction (see Chapter 2), but I had tried everything I could think of to help him, and nothing had worked. The impact on me and my children had become too much to bear. With tears streaming down my face, I packed a few of our belongings and loaded them into my car.

It was so hard to leave. You see, I still loved him – very much. Even after all the pain he had unknowingly inflicted on us, I loved him.

As I began the twelve–hour drive to my parent's house, I wondered if my old, rusty car would even make it that far. After I had driven for several hours, I rang Luke and told him we had left.

I no longer had the strength to fight for my marriage. I had to hand it all over to God. He would have to fight the battle for me. Later in the chapter, I will talk about how God graciously restored our marriage.

Bible Example

~ Rescue at the Red Sea ~

The story of the Red Sea is one of my favorite stories in the Bible. It describes God's miraculous intervention to save his people and it gives hope to us all.

The Israelites had been slaves to Egypt for four hundred years. After all their years of hardship, they cried out to God for help.

> The Israelites groaned in their slavery and cried out, and their cry for help because of their slavery went up to God. God heard their groaning and he remembered his covenant with Abraham, with Isaac and with Jacob. So God looked on the Israelites and was concerned about them. (Exodus 2:23–25 NIV)

To facilitate the rescue of the Israelites, God called Moses to return to Egypt and confront Pharoah to demand that he let the Israelites go (see chapter 10). Pharoah had no intention of allowing his slave workforce to leave. It was not until God had brought ten plagues (disasters) upon Egypt that Pharoah finally relented and let the Israelites go.

> Then the LORD said to Moses, "Tell the Israelites to turn back and encamp near Pi Hahiroth, between Migdol and the sea. They are to encamp by the sea, directly opposite Baal Zephon. Pharaoh will think, 'The Israelites are wandering around the land in confusion, hemmed in by the desert.' And I will

> harden Pharaoh's heart, and he will pursue them.
> But I will gain glory for myself through Pharaoh
> and all his army, and the Egyptians will know that
> I am the LORD." So the Israelites did this. (Exodus
> 14:1–3 NIV)

It is interesting that God purposefully led his people into a situation where it would take a miracle to survive. God warned the Israelites ahead of time that Pharoah would chase after them but promised to rescue them.

I wonder how often God leads us into situations where we have no choice but to trust him. I think it happens more often than we realize. By going through these times, we learn that God is trustworthy, and this helps our faith to grow.

As the Israelites looked up, they could see the entire Egyptian army marching after them. They were terrified and cried out to God for help.

> They said to Moses, "Was it because there were no
> graves in Egypt that you brought us to the desert to
> die? What have you done to us by bringing us out
> of Egypt? Didn't we say to you in Egypt, 'Leave us
> alone; let us serve the Egyptians'? It would have been
> better for us to serve the Egyptians than to die in the
> desert!'" Exodus 14:11–12 (NIV)

God spoke to his people through Moses, reassuring them that he would save them.

> Moses answered the people, "Do not be afraid. Stand
> firm and you will see the deliverance the LORD will
> bring you today. The Egyptians you see today you

will never see again. The Lord will fight for you; you need only to be still." Exodus 14:13–14 (NIV)

This mirrors God's promise to Jehoshaphat that God would fight the battle for him (see chapter 1). He wants to fight our battles too. All he asks is that we believe him and trust him. He will do the rest.

~ Take a Step Forward in Faith ~

God called the Israelites to step out in faith, even before they knew what God was going to do. He instructed Moses to tell the Israelites to move forward. Move where? They were hemmed in by the Red Sea in front of them and the Egyptian army behind them. God told them to start walking forward anyway.

When we take a step or two forward, even though we don't know God's specific plan, it demonstrates our faith in him. Then he intervenes to help us.

God illustrates this principle again when the Israelites were about to cross the Jordan River into the Promised Land (Joshua 3). It wasn't until the priests' toes touched the edge of the flooded river that God miraculously made the water stop flowing so they could walk across on dry land.

~ God Creates a Dry Path Through the Sea ~

God commands Moses:

> Raise your staff and stretch out your hand over the sea to divide the water so that the Israelites can go through the sea on dry ground. I will harden the hearts of the Egyptians so that they will go in after them. And I will gain glory through Pharaoh and

> all his army, through his chariots and his horsemen.
> The Egyptians will know that I am the LORD when
> I gain glory through Pharaoh, his chariots and his
> horsemen." (Exodus 14:16–18 NIV)

God protected the Israelites all night. The angel of God, which normally traveled in from of them moved and went behind them. The pillar of cloud also moved behind them. This brought darkness to the Egyptians and light to the Israelites. This prevented the Egyptians from coming any closer to them while God parted the waters.

> Then Moses stretched out his hand over the sea, and
> all that night the LORD drove the sea back with a
> strong east wind and turned it into dry land. The
> waters were divided, and the Israelites went through
> the sea on dry ground, with a wall of water on their
> right and on their left. (Exodus 14:21–22 NIV)

God miraculously created a dry path through the middle of the sea, with two giant walls of water on each side of the path. I can just imagine the Israelites rushed forward; no doubt terrified by the sight of the giant walls of water but rejoicing in God's miraculous rescue.

~ God Often Rescues Us at the Last Minute ~

As the last of the Israelites crossed the sea, the Egyptian army started pursuing them across the path.

> The Egyptians pursued them, and all Pharaoh's
> horses and chariots and horsemen followed them
> into the sea. During the last watch of the night the
> LORD looked down from the pillar of fire and cloud
> at the Egyptian army and threw it into confusion. He
> jammed the wheels of their chariots so that they had

difficulty driving. And the Egyptians said, "Let's get away from the Israelites! The LORD is fighting for them against Egypt." (Exodus 14:23–25 NIV)

Noticeably, God waits until "the last watch of the night" before he starts fighting against the Egyptians. The Bible contains many stories where God rescues his people at the last hour, and on some other occasions, when it appears he is too late. One such example is when Jesus raises Lazarus from the dead (Chapter 11). I can testify from my own life that this is often the way God works. Why does he do this? Because it stretches our faith and helps it to grow stronger.

~ The Enemy is Destroyed ~

Suddenly... God moved!

Then the LORD said to Moses, "Stretch out your hand over the sea so that the waters may flow back over the Egyptians and their chariots and horsemen." Moses stretched out his hand over the sea, and at daybreak the sea went back to its place. The Egyptians were fleeing toward it, and the LORD swept them into the sea. The water flowed back and covered the chariots and horsemen – the entire army of Pharaoh that had followed the Israelites into the sea. Not one of them survived. (Exodus 14:26–28 NIV)

God came through in time. All the Israelites were safe. It is one of the most amazing miracles recorded in the Bible.

And when the Israelites saw the mighty hand of the LORD displayed against the Egyptians, the people feared the LORD and put their trust in him and in Moses his servant. (Exodus 14:31 NIV)

Just as God had promised the Israelites, they would never see the Egyptians again. They were free.

Continuation of Personal Story

There were five essential components to the miraculous restoration of our marriage.

1. Prayer
2. Claiming God's promises
3. Healing
4. Repentance and Forgiveness
5. Gratitude

1. Prayer

I often brought our family situation to God in prayer. I prayed for Luke to stop drinking and I prayed for the restoration of our marriage. Though it took many years, I began to see gradual improvement.

2. Claiming God's Promises

I discovered the power of claiming God's promises in my own life.

In Jerry Savelle's teaching series called "The Hand of God," he taught from the Bible in Luke 18:1–8. This story is about a persistent widow who kept coming to a wicked judge, crying out to him "avenge me of my adversary." Jerry encouraged us to bring this Bible text before God and claim vengeance and restoration for the ways the devil had 'stolen' from us. For me personally, I applied this to recovery for Luke from his addiction and the complete restoration of our marriage.

Luke started to change right before my eyes. He didn't stop drinking right away, but his general disposition became calmer, less angry, more peaceful. Life started to become easier.

3. Healing

Before God healed Luke from his alcohol addiction, He first did a deep work in my own heart. God brought me to the place where I could be content even if Luke never stopped drinking. I accepted the reality that he may never change. However, it was precisely when I reached this point of surrender that God intervened and miraculously set Luke free (see Chapter 2). Our whole family was free. It has now been seven years since he stopped drinking and it stands as a testament to God's healing power.

4. Repentance and Forgiveness

Although Luke had expressed genuine remorse for his drinking and had asked me to forgive him, I only recently realized that I had not fully forgiven him.

As I began writing this book and sharing some of the painful stories from his drinking years, my dad wisely advised me to seek Luke's permission and consider the impact of my words. I realized that I had been holding onto his past mistakes and using them like a weapon against him. I repented before the Lord, sought his forgiveness, and asked for Luke's forgiveness. I finally released him from the weight of his past, truly setting him free.

5. Gratitude

Practicing gratitude is one of the most powerful tools we have in life. It can even make unbearable situations bearable.

Luke had tried many times to find a doctor who could help him to stop drinking but without success. He finally gave up trying. These were the darkest days of all. I managed to get him into a thirty–day rehab program. To be honest I thought our marriage was over. I was in a world of emotional pain and ready to walk away.

I am ashamed to admit that during that time I had thoughts of adultery. I was so lonely, so wounded, so desperate to feel loved. I longed to be held, to be comforted, to be told that I was beautiful and special. Praise God who made sure this never happened.

When I was talking to a friend about how I felt, they said something that probably saved our marriage. They said to write down all the things I loved about Luke and to read the list every day.

It was hard to get started, but through my tears, I slowly started to write. Before I knew it, I had written thirty things that I loved about him, and it really helped. Thinking of happier times and remembering the wonderful man I had married even brought a smile to my face, despite the heartache I felt.

I have now done this several times throughout our marriage and our life. As you deliberately choose to focus on what you are grateful for, there is a definite shift in your mind and heart. The positive mindset shift that the practice of gratitude brings is nothing short of miraculous.

Key Learnings from this Chapter

1. God can and will do the impossible, no matter how bad the situation looks.
2. God promises to fight our battles for us. Sometimes it happens quickly. Sometimes it takes many years, but God always comes through.

3. Even when you don't understand what God is doing, trust him anyway.

4. If you have been waiting a long time, don't give up. God will come through for you. It may feel like he rescues you at the last minute, but he will never be too late.

5. If you are struggling with your marriage, have hope that God can heal the relationship. From first–hand experience I know that troubled marriages can be restored, made whole and filled with love again.

Prayer

Dear Lord God, today I bring my _____ (*name your situation*) before you. You know the depths of my pain and heartache. I am unable to fix this situation by myself. It will take a miracle from you. Help me to keep holding on and keep trusting you to bring restoration to my life. In obedience to your Word, I choose to practice love, forgiveness, and gratitude. In Jesus' name, Amen.

Part 2

CHOOSE FAITH
OVER FEAR

Chapter Six

TRUST ME ONE DAY AT A TIME

How long will they refuse to believe in me, in spite of all the signs I have performed among them? (Numbers 14:11 NIV)

Personal Story

I had just started a new job. Within a day or two of starting, my new colleagues began telling me how hard things had been for them. They had been hired as temporary staff three months earlier. They were hired to support the three permanent staff to get through the busiest time of the year.

To their shock, a week after they started, all three of the permanent staff resigned. They told the new staff that the workload was just too much for them. They were exhausted from years of long days, working weekends, and not having lunch breaks. The two temporary staff members told me that they had been working ten to twelve hours per day, six days per week since they had started. They were stressed and utterly exhausted.

The manager who had employed me resigned on my second day on the job. There had been nine managers in the last two years. Something was seriously wrong. I started worrying about the job I had gotten myself into, despite feeling strongly that God had led me there.

I was already dealing with some mental health issues. I knew that I wouldn't be able to work these kinds of hours on an ongoing basis. Instead of trusting God, I spiraled into a state of severe depression and anxiety. Even though nothing bad had happened to me personally, I allowed feelings of anxiety and fear to consume me.

Despite my initial concerns, however, as I settled into the role, I found that I was really enjoying it. I was doing work I loved, and I was receiving lots of positive feedback from customers. While the role did present some challenges, I managed them by relying on God's grace and strength and taking it one day at a time. God faithfully provided me with the strength and health I needed each day.

It took me six months to realize that if I had trusted God from day one, I could have saved myself from those six weeks of depression and anxiety. Once again, God demonstrated that he always has our back. All we need to do is believe in him. When would I learn?

Bible Example

~ Spies Sent to the Promised Land ~

No matter how many times God miraculously rescued the Israelites, their faith and belief in him was always short-lived. They had winged and complained all the way from Egypt to the border of the Promised Land. God was about to make all their dreams come true.

Twelve men were sent to spy on the land and report back. Their report went as follows:

> We went into the land to which you sent us, and it does flow with milk and honey! Here is its fruit. But the people who live there are powerful, and the cities are fortified and very large. We even saw descendants of Anak there. (Numbers 13:27–28 NIV)

The people of Anak were giants.

> Then Caleb silenced the people before Moses and said, "We should go up and take possession of the land, for we can certainly do it." (Numbers 13:30 NIV)

> But the men who had gone up with him said, "We can't attack those people; they are stronger than we are." And they spread among the Israelites a bad report about the land they had explored. They said, "The land we explored devours those living in it. All the people we saw there are of great size." (Numbers 13:31–32 NIV)

They were looking at the giant people and giant cities in the Promised Land, instead of looking at their giant God. Despite seeing miracle after miracle with their own eyes, they still did not believe or trust God.

> That night all the members of the community raised their voices and wept aloud. All the Israelites grumbled against Moses and Aaron, and the whole assembly said to them, "If only we had died in Egypt! Or in this wilderness! Why is the LORD bringing us to this land only to let us fall by the sword? Our wives and children will be taken as plunder. Wouldn't it be better for us to go back to Egypt?" And they said to each other, "We should choose a leader and go back to Egypt." (Numbers 14:1–4 NIV)

In response, Joshua, and Caleb, two of the twelve spies, said:

> "The land we passed through and explored is exceedingly good. If the LORD is pleased with us, he will lead us into that land, a land flowing with milk and honey, and will give it to us. Only do not rebel against the LORD. And do not be afraid of the people of the land, because we will devour them. Their protection is gone, but the LORD is with us. Do not be afraid of them." (Numbers 14:7–9 NIV)

Out of the twelve men, only Joshua and Caleb trusted God to help them conquer the enemies in the Promised Land. They knew they couldn't do it in their own strength, but they had faith they could do it in God's strength.

The other ten spies convinced the rest of the Israelites that it couldn't be done. The giants were too big and there were too many of them. Despite witnessing God miraculously provide for them again and again, they still didn't trust him to fight for them and bring them into the Promised Land. This was the last straw for God.

> The Lord said to Moses, "How long will these people treat me with contempt? How long will they refuse to believe in me, in spite of all the signs I have performed among them?" (Numbers 14:11 NIV)

As a result, God pronounced judgment on them for their unbelief. The news was devastating.

> The Lord said to Moses and Aaron: "How long will this wicked community grumble against me? I have heard the complaints of these grumbling Israelites. So tell them, As surely as I live, declares the Lord, I

will do to you the very thing I heard you say: In this wilderness your bodies will fall—every one of you twenty years old or more who was counted in the census and who has grumbled against me. Not one of you will enter the land I swore with uplifted hand to make your home, except Caleb son of Jephunneh and Joshua son of Nun." (Numbers 14: 26–30 NIV)

This is how seriously God takes unbelief!

So the men Moses had sent to explore the land, who returned and made the whole community grumble against him by spreading a bad report about it— these men who were responsible for spreading the bad report about the land were struck down and died of a plague before the Lord. Of the men who went to explore the land, only Joshua son of Nun and Caleb son of Jephunneh survived. (Numbers 14:36–38 NIV)

God punished the ten men who caused the rest of the Israelites to sin by their unbelief. Then he made the people turn around and wander in the wilderness. They would wander around for forty years until all those who hadn't trusted God died. Afterward, God would bring their children into the Promised Land.

Throughout the forty years in the wilderness, Israel continued to grumble and complain, refusing to trust God.

Continuation of Personal Story

I had now been in my new role for nine months, and I'd been really enjoying it. As the busiest time of the year approached, however, I started to worry about what tasks I might be given to complete. The manager created a list of nearly two hundred tasks that needed to be completed in the next four weeks. Many were complicated and unfamiliar, and I could feel myself sinking back into anxiety and depression.

But once again, God intervened. Out of the two hundred tasks, I was only assigned three, and they were easy. God knew what I could manage, and he took care of me. When would I learn to trust God once and for all?

~ One Day at a Time ~

Living one day at a time was originally Jesus' idea. In Matthew 6:34 (NIV), Jesus said, "Therefore, do not worry about tomorrow, for tomorrow will worry about itself."

God gives us his grace and his strength one day at a time. He does not give us tomorrow's grace, today. He gives us his grace at precisely the time we need it.

Key Learnings from this Chapter

1. God takes unbelief very seriously. Don't be an unbelieving believer.
2. Even if everyone around you is full of doubt and unbelief, stay in faith.
3. God gives each one of us the grace and strength that we need, one day at a time.

Prayer

Lord, help me to believe you and put my trust in you, regardless of the circumstances (giants) I face. Even if those around me have given up on you, help me to trust you completely. Thank you for all the amazing ways you have led me in the past. As I recall these answers to prayer, please increase my faith and belief that you will help me in the current situation too. I choose to trust you, Jesus. In your Holy Name, Amen.

Chapter Seven

PRAISING GOD IN ADVANCE

Rejoice always, pray continually, give thanks in all circumstances; for this is God's will for you in Christ Jesus. (1 Thessalonians 5:16–18 NIV)

Personal story

It was 4.00 am and Luke and I were on our way to the airport for a much–anticipated beachside holiday. Suddenly the car started making loud noises and the lights on the dashboard flashed on and off. "Oh no," I thought, "not when we are on our way to catch a plane." Would we make it to the airport in time? Would we make it at all? Our hearts were pounding, not knowing what was going to happen. I started praying and praying.

This was one of the sudden "storms" that can occur in our lives. They are totally unexpected and come without warning. This incident reminds me of the story about Jesus and the storm.

Bible Example

~ Jesus and the Storm ~

The story is found in the Bible in Mark 4:35 through to Mark 5:1 (NIV). It had been a long day and Jesus and His disciples were tired.

They needed some rest and relaxation. Jesus said to them "Let us go over to the other side." (Mark 4:35 NIV). They got into a boat and began sailing across the lake.

One minute they were sailing calmly across the lake, and the next minute a furious storm came out of nowhere. The waves were crashing over the boat, and they thought they were going to drown.

> Jesus was in the stern, sleeping on a cushion. The disciples woke him and said to him, "Teacher, don't you care if we drown?" (Mark 4:38 NIV)

Many of these men were fishermen by trade. They had spent their lives on boats and had been through many storms. The fact that these seasoned sailors were terrified indicates that it must have been the biggest storm they had ever experienced. They thought they were going to die.

Jesus got up and simply spoke to the storm and in an instant, all was calm.

> He got up, rebuked the wind and said to the waves, "Quiet! Be still!" Then the wind died down and it was completely calm. (Mark 4:39 NIV)

Much to their relief, they reached the other side of the lake safely.

~ Faith in the Middle of Your Storm ~

> Jesus said to His disciples "Why are you so afraid? Do you still have no faith?" (Mark 4:40 NIV)

How do you think the disciples would have responded during the storm if they knew in advance that Jesus would keep them safe? If they had the benefit of hindsight, they would have known that they had nothing to worry about. Jesus would take care of them.

How could Jesus sleep through the storm? Because he knew that he would keep them safe, no matter how bad the storm was.

The challenge is when we are in the middle of our "storms" and we don't know how the story will end. This is when our faith in God needs to kick in. Faith means that while we are in the middle of a "storm" and we don't see the answer yet, we stay calm and peaceful, trusting God to take care of it.

~ Record the Stories of God's Faithfulness ~

As you go through life and encounter problems, write them down, pray about them, and give them to God. Stop worrying and wait to see how God will answer. When God does answer (and He always does), write down how he led you or what he did.

There is nothing so powerful for building up your faith than remembering the miraculous answers God has given you in the past. It's so exciting to go back and re-read your own stories of God's faithfulness. It becomes easier to put your faith in him the next time you are in the middle of a "storm."

As human beings, we forget the miraculous things God has done for us in the past. As I was preparing to write this book, I spent time going over journals from past years. I couldn't believe how much I had forgotten. Reading about the amazing ways God had led me in the past was very encouraging and it made my faith even stronger.

~ Peace that Passes Understanding ~

Philippians 4:6–7 (NIV) gives us this wonderful promise:

> Do not be anxious about anything, but in every
> situation, by prayer and petition, with thanksgiving,

present your requests to God. And the peace of God,
which transcends all understanding, will guard your
hearts and your minds in Christ Jesus.

When we are full of faith and hope in God in the middle of a "storm", the
peace that he gives us is miraculous. It is beyond our understanding.

I like the way the Living Bible expresses Philippians 4:6–7:

> Don't worry about anything; instead, pray about
> everything; tell God your needs, and don't forget to
> thank him for his answers. If you do this, you will
> experience God's peace, which is far more wonderful
> than the human mind can understand. His peace will
> keep your thoughts and your hearts quiet and at rest
> as you trust in Christ Jesus.

How many of us wish we could truly live like this? The wonderful
news is that you can. Trusting God is not based on feelings. It is a
decision you make. Regardless of what is going on in your life, no
matter how hopeless things look, when we choose to trust God, he
will give us his incredible peace.

Continuation of Personal Story

To our great relief, Luke and I managed to make it to our airport
parking service, but when we arrived, the engine of our car died.
There was no electrical power at all. We couldn't even open the trunk
to get our luggage out, and we couldn't even take the keys out of the
ignition.

When I went into the airport parking office and told them what had
happened, the attendant got angry with us and said, "Well you can't

leave the car there!" What were we supposed to do? We had to catch our plane!

Luke managed to get our luggage out of the trunk by folding down the back seats to access them. Thankfully, a second staff member came out to talk to us, who was much calmer and more reasonable than the first person. He said, "It's OK, go and catch your plane. Just ring roadside assistance when you have landed and get them to come out to look at the car. If they can't fix it, we'll get it towed to your mechanic." We were so grateful that the second parking attendant was understanding about our situation. We left the car there and managed to catch our plane on time.

I must admit I was a bit nervous about what might be wrong with my car. I had experienced a lot of trouble with it in the previous three years and had spent many thousands of dollars on repairs. No matter what they tried, no one seemed to be able to fix the car once and for all. But it hadn't played up for months. I thought it was finally fixed.

~ Things Quickly Go Downhill ~

We had an enjoyable holiday. We hadn't heard back from either the roadside assistance company or the airport parking company, so we had just assumed that the car was fixed, and all was well. Things quickly went downhill from there.

The day before we were due to leave to go home, I rang to confirm our flight reservations for the trip home. When I contacted the airline, they said they had canceled our flight and booked us on one three hours later. When I contacted the airport transfer bus, they were not able to take us any later, so it meant that we would have to wait at the airport for several more hours than planned.

When I contacted the airport parking service where our car had broken down, they said that it was still where we had left it; still not working; with the keys still stuck in the ignition! I couldn't believe it. When I rang the roadside assistance company, they said that they had not been able to locate the car (but they hadn't bothered to ring and tell us that). I logged a new job for them to come out and look at the car.

My heart started sinking.

~ The Power of Praise in the Middle of Trouble ~

It was at this point that I remembered the story of Jesus and the storm. Jesus said to his disciples "let us go over to the other side" (Mark 4:35 NIV). Sure enough, "they came to the other side of the sea" (Mark 5:1 AMP), but in between those two verses was the most terrifying storm. Only Jesus knew with certainty that they would make it safely across.

I reminded Luke of this Bible story and I said "Right now we are in the middle of the storm, but sometime in the next couple of days or weeks, my car will be fixed and safely back at home where it belongs. This 'storm' will be over."

Now I can't lie. I was feeling emotionally upset about the situation, but thankfully I remembered the power of thanking and praising God in advance, right in the middle of the trouble. This was a fairly new concept for me. I started praising God quietly, all the rest of that day and all the next day, while we were traveling home.

I rang the roadside assistance company, and they said they could not get my car going, so we asked them to arrange to tow it to our local mechanic. This would cost a lot, but we had no choice. Whenever fear came, I would start praising God again, trusting him to work it out.

When we got to the airport, we found that the airline had pushed our flight back another two hours, so we had to wait there all day.

When we finally boarded the plane and were taxiing down the runway ready to take off, one of the passengers came running down the back screaming "Let me off the plane, I have to get off." She was feeling sick and was very panicked. To our disbelief, we had to taxi back to the loading dock, re–open the main door, and let her off. Then the airline had to take all our luggage off to find the luggage belonging to this passenger, then reload our luggage back on.

We finally took off, but for the first hour, we experienced the worst turbulence I have ever experienced in my life. It was terrifying. The turbulence started to make me feel sick. I closed my eyes and kept taking deep breaths, trying to calm down my nervous system and trying not to vomit. The passengers around us were unusually noisy and we were sitting in the second back row, so people were coming and going to the toilet for the whole flight. It was an awful flight.

All this time, I kept quietly praising God in my heart. I remembered the importance of putting my faith in God in the middle of the "storm" when you don't know how the story will end. Nevertheless, I was still feeling emotionally exhausted.

About halfway through the flight, I said to God "I'm sorry, I'm exhausted. I hardly have any praise left in me." Honesty, I just felt like screaming and crying, but I knew I had to "hold it together" until we landed.

I remembered the Bible text in Ephesians 6:13 (AMPC):

> Therefore put on God's complete armor, that you may be able to resist and stand your ground on the evil day [of danger], and, having done all [the crisis demands], to stand [firmly in your place].

So I stayed firm in faith, even though I felt at breaking point. I had praised God continually, until I could finally do no more than to stand firmly in my place, trusting God to work on my behalf. We finally arrived home and dropped into bed around 3.00 am.

I slept in late the next morning and when I got up, Luke said "Your car is fixed." I couldn't believe my ears. Out of all the potential things that could have gone wrong, all it had needed was a new battery. The very next morning, my car was parked safely at home, just like I had said (by faith) that it would be. The "storm" was over.

I had thought it might take days or weeks to fix (as it had in the past), but it was fixed in just a couple of hours. Like the story where Jesus calms the storm, we had arrived "safely on the other side."

~ Resting in Jesus ~

I belong to a ladies' prayer and support group, and a week later, I told one of the ladies about what had happened. She helped me to see that trusting God and praising him in our "storms" should not be a huge effort, but rather, we should simply rest in Jesus' care, knowing that he will take care of us. I immediately started putting this into practice. It is wonderful. It really helps you to stay calm and peaceful.

This is why Jesus was able to sleep in the boat in the middle of a huge storm. He was completely at rest, knowing that all would be well.

Key Learnings from this Chapter

1. When we go through "storms" in life, remember the story of Jesus and the storm. Even though things looked really bad, they had nothing to worry about. Jesus would keep them safe.
2. When you are going through a "storm", pray first and then start praising and thanking God in advance. The Bible calls this a "sacrifice of praise" (Hebrews 13:15 NIV). This is because when we are in the middle of a "storm" and have no

idea how the story will end, it is a "sacrifice" (i.e., it feels hard) to praise God in the middle of it.

3. When we praise God during times of trouble, it honors him and demonstrates our faith. This pleases him.

4. Praising God in trouble is not a feeling you have. It is a decision you make.

5. The "storm" will eventually end. Learn to rest in Jesus while you are going through the "storm", just as Jesus had slept peacefully on the boat.

6. Jesus' first question to his disciples was "Why are you so afraid? Where is your faith?" This is Jesus' question to us too. Jesus is telling us that even during the worst "storms" of our lives, he is with us. Trust him and do not give into fear.

Prayer

Precious Lord Jesus, I give all of life's "storms" into your care. I choose to trust you completely. I praise you for all the times you have kept me safe in the past. By faith, I know that you will take care of this storm too. Thank you for your peace, Amen.

Chapter Eight

STOP DOUBTING
AND BELIEVE

Jesus said to Thomas "Stop doubting and believe!"
(John 20:27 NIV)

Personal Story

When our third child, a little girl, was born, the doctors informed us that she had a very serious health condition, along with potential secondary health issues.

The pediatrician who delivered the news about our daughter's medical condition had no bedside manners at all. He bluntly announced how severe our daughter's condition was and then said, "There is nothing that you could have done about it, and there is nothing you can do." Then he left the room. My husband, Luke, and I were speechless and left in complete shock. He didn't give us any information about our daughter's health condition. He didn't wait to answer any of our questions. We wondered about the future of our precious daughter and how we could support her.

Finally, the day came to take her home from the hospital. On the way home, we had the Christian radio playing. The Bible verse that came on the radio was, "We know that in all things God works for the good of those who love him." (Romans 8:28 NIV). I found this Bible promise a source of comfort and I clung to it every time doubt or fear would arise in my mind. Nevertheless, worry and anxiety still plagued my mind when I contemplated her uncertain future.

Then my sister gave me some valuable advice. She suggested that I try to focus on one day at a time instead of worrying about the unknown future. She said, 'Ask yourself, "Can I handle her today?"' The answer was always "Yes, of course we could handle her today". She was the most beautiful, precious baby girl. As I continued this daily practice, it really helped. I refused to worry about the future and learned to trust God one day at a time.

In this chapter, we will explore some examples of Jesus helping people who needed a miracle of healing.

Bible Example

~ Story 1: Jesus Heals the Blind and the Mute ~

> As Jesus went on from there, two blind men followed
> him, calling out, "Have mercy on us, Son of David!"
> When he had gone indoors, the blind men came to
> him, and He asked them, "Do you believe that I am
> able to do this?" "Yes, Lord," they replied. Then he
> touched their eyes and said, "According to your faith
> let it be done to you," and their sight was restored."
> (Matthew 9:27–30 NIV)

Jesus' first question was, "Do you believe I can do this?" They didn't say "I think so," or "I hope so," they said with confidence "Yes Lord." Two simple words that declared their unwavering faith in Jesus. Then Jesus touched their eyes and instantly they could see.

It's interesting that Jesus doesn't say "According to my faith, let it be done to you." He says, "According to your faith let it be done to you." Jesus meets us at whatever level our faith is at.

~ Story 2: The Faith of the Centurion ~

When Jesus had entered Capernaum, a centurion came to him, asking for help. "Lord," he said, "my servant lies at home paralyzed, suffering terribly." Jesus said to him, "Shall I come and heal him?" The centurion replied, "Lord, I do not deserve to have you come under my roof. But just say the word, and my servant will be healed."

When Jesus heard this, he was amazed and said to those following him, "Truly I tell you, I have not found anyone in Israel with such great faith." Then Jesus said to the centurion, "Go! Let it be done just as you believed it would." And his servant was healed at that moment." (Matthew 8:5–8,10,13 NIV)

This man wasn't even a member of the church. He was a Roman soldier, yet he had unwavering faith in Jesus.

Notice Jesus' words to the man in Matthew 8:13 (NIV) "Go! Let it be done just as you believed it would." This shows us that the key to accessing Jesus' miracle–working power is to believe.

The centurion believed that just a word from Jesus would heal his servant, and Jesus honored what he believed. Jesus was amazed at the centurion's faith. Once Jesus spoke, the servant was healed immediately.

~ Story 3 and 4: Jesus Rises a Dead
Girl and Heals a Sick Woman ~

> One of the synagogue leaders, named Jairus, came,
> and when he saw Jesus, he fell at his feet. He pleaded
> earnestly with him, "My little daughter is dying.
> Please come and put your hands on her so that she
> will be healed and live." So Jesus went with him."
> (Mark 5:22–24 NIV)

In this story, Jairus believed that he needed Jesus to come and physically lay his hands on his sick daughter. Jesus honored what the synagogue leader believed and agreed to go with him to heal his daughter. On the way, they were interrupted by someone else who needed a miracle.

> A large crowd followed and pressed around him. And
> a woman was there who had been subject to bleeding
> for twelve years. She had suffered a great deal under
> the care of many doctors and had spent all she had,
> yet instead of getting better she grew worse. When
> she heard about Jesus, she came up behind him in the
> crowd and touched his cloak, because she thought, "If
> I just touch his clothes, I will be healed." Immediately
> her bleeding stopped and she felt in her body that she
> was freed from her suffering. (Mark 5:24–29 NIV)

This woman didn't even ask Jesus to heal her. She believed that all she had to do was touch his clothes, and instantly she was healed.

> At once Jesus realized that power had gone out from
> him. He turned around in the crowd and asked, "Who
> touched my clothes?" "You see the people crowding
> against you," his disciples answered, "and yet you can
> ask, 'Who touched me?'" But Jesus kept looking around

to see who had done it. Then the woman, knowing
what had happened to her, came and fell at his feet and,
trembling with fear, told him the whole truth. He said
to her, "Daughter, your faith has healed you. Go in peace
and be freed from your suffering." (Mark 5:30–34 NIV)

Again, Jesus did not say my faith has healed you. He said your faith
has healed you. Jesus' miracle–working power worked exactly in line
with what she believed.

While Jesus was still speaking, some people came
from the house of Jairus, the synagogue leader. "Your
daughter is dead," they said. "Why bother the teacher
anymore?" (Mark 5:35 NIV)

The people from Jairus' house thought that because the girl was dead,
it was all over. Jesus had compassion for the girl's father, knowing that
his faith might falter, so he encouraged him to keep believing.

Overhearing what they said, Jesus told him, "Don't
be afraid; just believe" (Mark 5:36 NIV)

In the Amplified Bible, Classic Edition, this verse reads:

Overhearing but ignoring what they said, Jesus said
to the ruler of the synagogue, "Do not be seized with
alarm and struck with fear; only keep on believing."
(Mark 5:36 AMPC)

Are you believing for a miracle, but the people around you are talking
in unbelief and your faith has started to waver? Perhaps like Jairus, you
started off needing one type of miracle (healing his sick daughter)
and then the situation seriously worsens (she dies). Now he needs an
even bigger miracle. This is like the story of Lazarus (see chapter 11).

Even when it feels that all your hopes have been dashed, Jesus' message is still the same. Don't be afraid. Keep on believing!

> When he arrived at the house of Jairus, he did not let anyone go in with him except Peter, John and James, and the child's father and mother. Meanwhile, all the people were wailing and mourning for her. "Stop wailing," Jesus said. "She is not dead but asleep." They laughed at him, knowing that she was dead. But he took her by the hand and said, "My child, get up!" Her spirit returned, and at once she stood up. Then Jesus told them to give her something to eat. Her parents were astonished. (Luke 8:51–56 NIV)

Why did Jesus only take Peter, John, James, and the child's parents inside? Because he only wanted those who believed in his miracle–working power to be present. Jesus simply took the little girl's hand and tells her to get up and instantly she is raised from the dead.

If you are facing an impossible situation today and asking God for a miracle, be careful about whom you spend time with. Make sure that you spend time with people who will build up your faith, and who are willing to believe for the impossible with you.

~ Story 5: Jesus Heals a Demon–Possessed Boy ~

> When they came to the crowd, a man approached Jesus and knelt before him. "Lord, have mercy on my son," he said. "He has seizures and is suffering greatly. He often falls into the fire or into the water. I brought him to your disciples, but they could not heal him." "You unbelieving and perverse generation," Jesus replied, "How long shall I stay with you? How long shall I put up with you? Bring the boy here to me." Jesus rebuked

the demon, and it came out of the boy, and he was
healed at that moment. (Matthew 17:14–18 NIV)

Take notice of the next two verses:

> Then the disciples came to Jesus in private and
> asked, "Why couldn't we drive it out?" He replied,
> "Because you have so little faith. Truly I tell you, if
> you have faith as small as a mustard seed, you can
> say to this mountain, 'Move from here to there,' and
> it will move. Nothing will be impossible for you."
> (Matthew 17:19–20 NIV)

Jesus told his disciples that the main problem was their lack of faith.
He went on to explain how powerful even a tiny amount of faith is.

~ Our Lack of Faith Limits God ~

Jesus and His disciples went back to visit his hometown of Nazareth.
The people in Nazareth had seen Jesus grow up there. They knew him
as the local carpenter. They did not believe that he was the Son of God
or that he was even a prophet.

> Jesus said to them, "A prophet is not without honor
> except in his own town and in his own home." And
> he did not do many miracles there because of their
> lack of faith. (Matthew 13:57–58 NIV)

From these stories, we have seen the incredible miracles that Jesus will
do for people who believe. We have also seen how our unbelief limits
God's ability to work on our behalf. In Matthew 21:22 (NIV) Jesus
says, "If you believe, you will receive whatever you ask for in prayer."

We can expect the same miracle–working power of Jesus today. Jesus
said:

> Very truly I tell you, whoever believes in me will do
> the works I have been doing, and they will do even
> greater things than these, because I am going to the
> Father. (John 14:12 NIV)

Remember that Jesus meets us at the level our faith is at. Jairus believed that Jesus had to physically touch his daughter to heal her. The centurion believed that just a simple word from Jesus was enough. The woman with the issue of blood believed that she would be healed by touching Jesus' clothes.

Each one of them received exactly what they believed.

Continuation of Personal Story

I poured my love into our precious daughter every day. Each time we came to a milestone in her life that we had been worried about, she sailed through it.

The only major health issue we had to deal with was when she was five years old. She started waking up through the night with severe pain in her legs.

When we took her to the children's hospital, they informed us that she needed a major operation to rebuild her legs so that she could keep walking. They said that if we didn't do the surgery, she would be in a wheelchair for the rest of her life. We agreed to do the surgery.

Our little girl didn't let anything stop her. The doctors had said that the entire process of rebuilding her legs could take up to two years, yet our daughter was fully healed in six months. The doctors said it would take three months for her to learn to walk again, but she surprised everyone by learning to walk in just two weeks!

When we were worried about her being teased at school, she flourished. When we held her 21st birthday party, she was surrounded by a huge group of friends who obviously loved her. Now she has found a wonderful partner to share her life with.

God is so good. All the things we were worried about when she was born, simply didn't happen. She is a happy, well–adjusted young woman with a great future ahead.

Key Learnings from this Chapter

1. Our belief in Jesus is of utmost importance.
2. God specializes in doing the impossible. Keep believing and see what God will do.
3. If you are believing God for a miracle, surround yourself with believers. Don't spend time with people who are full of doubt.
4. God's miracles are available just as much today as they were when Jesus was on the earth.
5. Trust God one day at a time. He gives His grace and strength for each day.

Prayer

Dear Lord, please forgive me for doubting you. Help me to keep believing in your miracle–working power, no matter how things look. Even if circumstances appear to get worse, help me to keep trusting you. There is no circumstance too great for you. I declare that I believe. In Jesus' Name, Amen.

Part 3

SOMETIMES THINGS GET WORSE BEFORE THEY GET BETTER

Chapter Nine

KEEP BELIEVING IN YOUR DREAM

Take delight in the Lord, and he will give you the desires of your heart. (Psalm 37:4 NIV)

Personal Story

I thought I had it made.

I had worked hard in my career and had successfully gained a position at the National Office of one of the country's largest companies. This meant that we would be packing up our lives and moving to another state. This was huge. It's what I'd always dreamed of.

Just five short years later, my whole world came crashing down. I found myself in the hospital, unable to function at all. I couldn't sleep. I couldn't work. I couldn't look after my children. What had happened to my dreams? They felt so far away, they may as well have been on another planet.

This ordeal reminds me of the story of Joseph in the Bible. His dreams looked impossible too.

Bible Example

~ God Gives Joseph a Dream ~

When Joseph was a young man, God gave him two dreams, showing him that one day he would be a ruler. The dreams felt so significant and so real that Joseph told his father and his brothers about them. They were not impressed, to say the least.

Their father made no secret of the fact that Joseph was his favorite child. In fact, he made Joseph a special, colorful coat that symbolized that he was the prince among his brothers. As a result, his brothers hated him. Joseph's dreams just added fuel to the fire.

From time to time, Jacob sent Joseph out to check on his brothers, and in the past, he had brought back a bad report about them. Over the years, their hatred for Joseph grew stronger and stronger.

The next time Jacob sent Joseph to go and check on his brothers, they threw him into a deep pit. They made fun of him and ignored his cries for help. Some of them wanted to kill him. As they were discussing what to do with him, some Ishmaelites came along the road on their way to Egypt. Joseph's brothers decided to sell Joseph to the Ishmaelites as a slave. Joseph was only seventeen years old.

What a long, lonely journey it must have been all the way to Egypt. Where were the dreams God had put in his heart? Despite his circumstances, Joseph clung to God and stayed faithful to him. He clung to his dreams too, even though they now looked impossible.

~ God Begins Joseph's Training to
Become Ruler of Egypt ~

Thankfully, Joseph was bought by a good man named Potiphar, who was captain of Pharoah's guards. As Joseph faithfully went about his duties, it soon became obvious to Potiphar that God blessed everything that Joseph did.

> The Lord was with Joseph so that he prospered, and he lived in the house of his Egyptian master. When his master saw that the Lord was with him and that the Lord gave him success in everything he did, Joseph found favor in his eyes and became his attendant. Potiphar put him in charge of his household, and he entrusted to his care everything he owned. (Genesis 39:2–6)

Even though Joseph was now a slave in a foreign country, the Lord was still with him. He blessed him and gave him success in everything he did. As a result, Joseph found favor with Potiphar, and he put Joseph in charge of everything he owned.

We can all take heart from this. Even in the hardest of times, when we don't understand what God is doing, he is still with us. He is still in control. He will even bless us right in the middle of our greatest challenges.

While God's ultimate purposes remained veiled until later in life, he utilized the opportunity of managing Potiphar's household to begin training Joseph to be the future ruler of Egypt. Through this experience, God taught Joseph essential skills such as managing resources, managing people, and making wise decisions. God was also developing his maturity of character.

~ The Next Stage of Joseph's Training ~

Just when it started to look like life in Egypt wouldn't be so bad after all, Potiphar's wife falsely accused Joseph of trying to rape her. When Potiphar came home, he believed his wife rather than Joseph and threw him in prison.

> Joseph's master took him and put him in prison, the place where the king's prisoners were confined. But while Joseph was there in the prison, the Lord was with him; he showed him kindness and granted him favor in the eyes of the prison warden. So the warden put Joseph in charge of all those held in the prison, and he was made responsible for all that was done there. (Genesis 39:20–23 NIV)

What a blow. He had gone from being a lowly slave and had worked his way up to being the head of Potiphar's household. Now, based on one false accusation, he found himself in prison.

Sometimes things get worse before they get better.

Can you imagine the thoughts that must have been going through Joseph's mind? It would have been so easy to accuse God of abandoning him all over again. Remarkably, instead of giving into doubt, depression, and utter despair, Joseph kept clinging to his faith in God.

When we hit rock bottom, is it possible that God is still firmly in control? That somehow out of this awful situation, God can bring meaning and purpose and even bless us beyond our wildest dreams?

Now that takes faith!

Joseph stayed faithful to God and God blessed him by giving him favor with the prison warden. The prison warden put Joseph in charge of the entire prison.

This is the second stage of Joseph's training to be the ruler of Egypt. God used the opportunity of working for Potiphar to give Joseph valuable training in managing a large household. Now it was time to train Joseph how to manage a large, complex organization – a prison.

Joseph must have often thought about the dreams he had as a teenager. They were treasured deep in his heart. He must have wondered how they could possibly come to fruition now that he was not only a slave in a foreign country, but now in prison. Despite all this, Joseph continued to trust and obey God.

God was working behind the scenes, putting everything in place for Joseph's divine destiny. He was equipping Joseph with invaluable experience and knowledge, molding him into the future ruler of Egypt.

~ God Speaks Using Dreams Again ~

Two years later, two of Pharoah's most esteemed servants – his butler and baker – were thrown into the same prison as Joseph. While they were there, they both had dreams on the same night. When Joseph came to check on them, he saw that they were dejected and asked them what was wrong. They told him that they had both had dreams the previous night but didn't know their meaning. God gave Joseph the interpretation of their dreams and the interpretation came true.

Again, God was using dreams in Joseph's life. Though his own dreams looked like they were never going to happen, Joseph was still willing for God to use him to help others interpret their dreams.

Joseph told the butler that he would be released from prison in three days. Then he asks him a favor. He said:

> But when all goes well with you, remember me, and
> show me kindness; mention me to Pharaoh and get
> me out of this prison. I was forcibly carried off from
> the land of the Hebrews, and even here I have done
> nothing to deserve being put in a dungeon. (Genesis
> 40:14–15)

But the butler forgets all about him. Another devastating blow.

~ Joseph's Training is Complete ~

When two full years had passed, Pharaoh had a dream. (Genesis 41:1 NIV)

Two years later, Pharoah himself had a troubling dream and couldn't find anyone to interpret it for him. At this time, the butler remembers Joseph and recommends him to Pharoah. Pharoah sends for Joseph immediately.

Once God's timing is right, things can happen very quickly. God had finished Joseph's training. His dreams were about to come true.

God gave Joseph the meaning of Pharoah's dream. He explained that God was showing Pharoah what was about to happen. There were going to be seven years of great abundance, followed by seven years of extreme famine. Not only did God give Joseph the interpretation of the dream, but he also gave him wise counsel for Pharoah about how to handle the situation.

~ Joseph Becomes Ruler of Egypt ~

The plan seemed good to Pharaoh and to all his officials. So, Pharaoh asked them, "Can we find anyone like this man, one in whom is the spirit of God?" Then Pharaoh said to Joseph, "Since God has made all this known to you, there is no one so discerning and wise as you. You shall be in charge of my palace, and all my people are to submit to your orders. Only with respect to the throne will I be greater than you." So Pharaoh said to Joseph, "I hereby put you in charge of the whole land of Egypt." (Genesis 41:37–41 NIV)

God's timing was perfect. God had finally finished Joseph's training and now brought his dreams to fruition. Joseph was thirty years old. He had been a slave for thirteen years.

Second Corinthians 5:7 (NIV) says, "For we live by faith, not by sight."

This means that no matter how things look, no matter how we feel, we should take no notice. Keep your faith in God. Remind yourself that God is always in control.

~ God Had Placed Joseph in the
Right Place at the Right Time ~

God had placed Joseph in the right place at the right time.

First, he took Joseph to Egypt where he would eventually become the ruler. There, Joseph learned the language and customs of the Egyptians. God arranged it so that Joseph was sold to Potiphar, a good man, and a high-ranking official in Egypt. God gave Joseph favor with Potiphar, who put Joseph in charge of his entire household.

When Joseph was falsely accused and thrown into prison, he wasn't just thrown in any old prison. He was put in the prison where the king's prisoners were kept. This is important. Because Joseph was being held in this particular prison, God arranged for him to meet Pharoah's butler. God gave the butler a dream and gave Joseph the correct interpretation. God then gave Pharoah two dreams, and he could not find anyone to interpret them. Then the butler remembered Joseph. Joseph was brought to Pharoah to interpret his dream. God also gave Joseph wise counsel for Pharoah. God had arranged for Joseph to have just the right training that he needed. Suddenly, God's perfect plan came together.

God really is "The God of the impossible."

~ What the Enemy Meant for Harm,
God Meant for Good ~

The story goes on to say that the famine impacted the whole world, including where Joseph's family lived. Eventually, his brothers came to Egypt to buy food. They bowed down before Joseph, just as they had in his dreams. They did not recognize him. Later, Joseph revealed himself to his brothers. He told them not to feel bad that they sold him as a slave because it was all part of God's master plan.

> And now, do not be distressed and do not be angry with yourselves for selling me here, because it was to save lives that God sent me ahead of you. For two years now there has been famine in the land, and for the next five years there will be no plowing and reaping. But God sent me ahead of you to preserve for you a remnant on earth and to save your lives by a great deliverance. So then, it was not you who sent me here, but God. He made me father to Pharaoh, lord of his entire household and ruler of all Egypt. (Genesis 45:5–8 NIV)

God had been leading and guiding Joseph the whole time. If you are going through a difficult time, it can really help you if you recall the Bible promise in Romans 8:28 (NIV):

> And we know that in all things God works for the good of those who love him, who have been called according to his purpose.

Continuation of Personal Story

During my time in the hospital, I was very ill. I couldn't even communicate with other people. I couldn't comprehend a word they were saying. It felt as if they were speaking a foreign language, even though they were just using regular English. I would nod my head from time to time, to make it appear as though I was following along, but in reality, I could not understand a word they said. It was such a frightening experience. Eventually, I was diagnosed with Post Natal Depression.

Thankfully our close friends from church stepped in to care for our precious children as my husband Luke was self–employed and couldn't take any time off.

With good care, therapy, and medicine, I started to show improvement, and after three weeks, I was able to return home. It was such a relief to have our family reunited, but I was still not well enough to resume work.

After three years at home, with continued therapy and medicine, I was finally well enough to go back to work, but I was uncertain about what kind of work I could do. I had enjoyed a successful career before having a family and before being sick, but my career had not taken a traditional path. Although I had advanced quickly, I had missed out on many of the fundamentals of my profession. I wondered if I would have to start over from scratch and get a graduate position. I prayed every day that God would lead me to the right job.

One area of work I was comfortable with was writing policies and procedures. I decided to focus on jobs that required these skills. What God did next was truly miraculous.

I received a phone call to go in for a job interview for a policy and procedures position in a large government department. During the interview, when the manager had finished reading my resume, to my surprise, she said "Maybe you'd like my job. I'm leaving soon and we have just advertised my job too". I couldn't believe my ears! When she described her job, I agreed that it sounded like a job I would really enjoy. After a second job interview with the manager and the Chief Financial Officer, they offered me the job.

In my wildest dreams, I could not have imagined getting such a prestigious position, after not working for the past three years. I loved the job. To this day, I look back on this as being the best job I have ever had. I've never had a job like it since. It felt like it was a beautiful present that God had given me after all the difficult years I had been through.

Has God put a dream in your heart, but it feels like it's never going to happen? Are you tempted to give up on your dreams? I encourage you not to give up on your dreams. Keep believing and at the right time, God will bring them to pass.

Key Learnings from this Chapter

1. God has a special future planned for each one of us.
2. God puts dreams in our hearts and brings them to pass in His perfect timing.
3. No matter what we are going through, no matter how dismal or how impossible it seems, keep trusting in God and his plan for your life.
4. God will give you favor with others, even unbelievers.
5. God uses difficulties to train us and to build maturity of faith and character.

Prayer

Dear Lord, when life is hard, please help me to trust that you are still in control. Thank you for the dreams you have put in my heart. I trust you to bring them to pass in your perfect timing. Thank you that you use our difficulties to train and prepare us for the dreams you have put in our hearts. In Jesus' Name, Amen.

Chapter Ten

FREEDOM FROM BONDAGE

> The Lord said, "I have indeed seen the misery of my people in Egypt. I have heard them crying out because of their slave drivers, and I am concerned about their suffering. So I have come down to rescue them from the hand of the Egyptians." (Exodus 3:7–10 NIV)

Have you been in bondage to a painful situation for a long time? Take heart, God will not leave you there. He will rescue you. He rescued me.

Personal Story

I know what it's like to be in bondage. I was in bondage to the debilitating illness of OCD (obsessive–compulsive disorder) from the age of nine.

I knew something was drastically wrong. Recently, every time I walked home from school, I felt this strong compulsion to walk backwards and forwards over the same patch of concrete path, a certain number of times. "How embarrassing," I thought to myself. "I hope no one sees me."

I knew that logically, it did not make sense, but I just couldn't help it. I had an overwhelming fear that if I didn't do it, something really bad would happen. If I did do it, I felt everything would be fine.

My behavior quickly escalated. I started counting everything I did, such as counting how many turns it took to turn the shower on and off. Next, I started with 'counting rituals'. If I was sitting at the dining room table and mum called me to come into the kitchen, I could not get up from the table until I had completed my 'counting rituals.' The illness was becoming more and more debilitating. It was completely taking over my life.

But God did a miracle to free me from this bondage. I will elaborate on this later in the chapter.

Bible Example

~ God Calls Moses to Rescue the Israelites ~

God's people, the Israelites, were also in bondage. They had been slaves in Egypt for four hundred years. In this chapter, we read how God frees His people from bondage to Egypt.

> And now the cry of the Israelites has reached me, and I have seen the way the Egyptians are oppressing them. So now, go. I am sending you to Pharaoh to bring my people the Israelites out of Egypt. (Exodus 3:9–10 NIV)

God told Moses that he was sending him to go and rescue his chosen people, Israel, from bondage to Egypt. The only trouble is – Moses didn't want to go.

Not that I blame him. It was a daunting task, to be sure. But as always, when God asks us to do something, He promises to be with us and to help us. God never calls us to do anything without providing all that we need to carry out the task.

~ Moses Raised in Pharoah's Palace ~

Moses had been raised as a prince in Pharoah's palace through some divinely orchestrated circumstances. He was raised in a life of privilege and wealth, even though he was actually an Israelite.

Even as a young man, Moses knew that God was calling him to save the Israelites.

One day, Moses saw an Egyptian beating an Israelite. Moses intervened in the fight and killed the Egyptian. He thought he was doing the will of God to help his people. When Pharoah found out what Moses had done, he wanted to kill Moses. Moses ran for his life.

He settled a long way away, in the desert. He had been there for forty years when God called him to return to Egypt to rescue his people. He was no longer the self–confident young man he had once been. He was rusty about the language and customs of Egypt. He also had a debilitating illness in the form of a significant speech impediment.

Moses gave God every excuse he could think of as to why he can't do what God is asking. The thing he was most worried about was his speech impediment. He couldn't speak well. How could he possibly take on a role where he had to speak to Israel's leaders and to Pharoah himself? It felt like an impossible task.

To encourage Moses, God shows him some miraculous signs. He told Moses to perform these miraculous signs for the leaders of the Israelites and for Pharoah, to establish his credibility that God had really called him. Finally, Moses said, "Pardon your servant, Lord. Please send someone else." (Exodus 4:13 NIV)

God got angry with Moses then. Why was God angry? Because of Moses' unbelief and his lack of trust that God would help him.

> Then the LORD's anger burned against Moses, and he said, "What about your brother, Aaron the Levite? I know he can speak well. He is already on his way to meet you, and he will be glad to see you. You shall speak to him and put words in his mouth; I will help both of you speak and will teach you what to do. He will speak to the people for you, and it will be as if he were your mouth and as if you were God to him. But take this staff in your hand so you can perform the signs with it." (Exodus 4:14–17 NIV)

God knew perfectly well about Moses' speech impediment. After all, he had created Moses. God had already put a plan in place to help Moses. Moses' brother Aaron was an excellent public speaker. God had already spoken to Aaron and told him to go and meet Moses in the desert.

No matter what God calls us to do He will always provide the help and resources we will need to carry out the task successfully.

~ God Calls Me to Lead a Bible Study Group ~

I experienced this when my eldest daughter was a baby, and I was part of a local Mother's Group. God had planted the idea in my heart that he wanted me to run a Bible study group for my local Mother's Group. I was afraid to initiate this. I didn't want them to dislike me or to think that I was "preaching at them."

I didn't know how to go about it or what to say. God gave me the courage to tell one of the mums what God had put on my heart, and to my surprise and delight, she said that she was a Christian too. She encouraged me to start the group and said that she would be there to support me. When I was fearful, God provided someone to help me. I was so grateful.

God gave me the courage to ask the other mums, and to my delight, several of the mums accepted the invitation. We had a wonderful time together. It was such a joy, not only sharing the journey of being new mums together but also sharing our faith and supporting each other in a whole new way.

God is so faithful.

~ Moses and Aaron Approach Pharoah ~

Reluctantly, Moses agreed to do what God was asking. He went to meet his brother, Aaron in the desert and they went back to Egypt together. They told the elders of the Israelites that God was going to rescue them. They also showed them the miraculous signs. Just as God had promised, the elders believed Moses and Aaron. They greatly rejoiced that God had not forgotten them. He was going to rescue them.

Then Moses and Aaron went to Pharoah and told him that God wanted him to let the Israelites go. What was the first thing Pharoah did? He made the work infinitely harder for the Israelites.

> But the king of Egypt said, "Moses and Aaron, why are you taking the people away from their labor? Get back to your work!" Then Pharaoh said, "Look, the people of the land are now numerous, and you are stopping them from working."

> That same day Pharaoh gave this order to the slave drivers and overseers in charge of the people: "You are no longer to supply the people with straw for making bricks; let them go and gather their own straw. But require them to make the same number of bricks as before; don't reduce the quota. They are lazy; that is

why they are crying out, 'Let us go and sacrifice to our God.' Make the work harder for the people so that they keep working and pay no attention to lies." (Exodus 5:4–9 NIV)

Sometimes things get much worse just before they get better.

The Israelite overseers realized they were in trouble when they were told, "You are not to reduce the number of bricks required of you for each day." When they left Pharaoh, they found Moses and Aaron waiting to meet them, and they said, "May the LORD look on you and judge you! You have made us obnoxious to Pharaoh and his officials and have put a sword in their hand to kill us." (Exodus 5:19–21 NIV)

Now, not only did Moses have Pharoah against him, but now the Israelites were also against him. They blamed him for the harsh burden Pharoah had laid on them. Moses cried out to the Lord.

Then the LORD said to Moses, "Now you will see what I will do to Pharaoh: Because of my mighty hand he will let them go; because of my mighty hand he will drive them out of his country." (Exodus 6:1 NIV)

Moses reported this to the Israelites, but they did not listen to him because of their discouragement and harsh labor. (Exodus 6:9 NIV)

How do we react when we believe we have a promise from God to help us and then our circumstances get worse instead of better? It tests our faith at a whole new level. Why does God test our faith? To help it grow stronger. It becomes more important than ever to cling to the promises of God. Remember the Bible definition of faith:

> Faith is confidence in what we hope for and assurance
> about what we do not see. (Hebrews 11:1 NIV)

We hope for something. We cannot see it happening yet, but we have confidence that God will bring it to pass. Second Corinthians 5:7 (NIV) says "For we live by faith not by sight."

This means that we keep trusting God no matter what our circumstances look like. By faith, we know that God will keep his promise to us.

~ Free at Last ~

Moses and Aaron continued to ask Pharoah to let the Israelites go. God sent one devastating plague (disaster) after another upon Egypt. Finally, after the tenth plague, when Egypt was almost completely ruined, Pharoah finally agreed to let the Israelites go.

> The Egyptians urged the people to hurry and leave the
> country. "For otherwise," they said, "we will all die!"
> So the people took their dough before the yeast was
> added, and carried it on their shoulders in kneading
> troughs wrapped in clothing. The Israelites did as
> Moses instructed and asked the Egyptians for articles
> of silver and gold and for clothing. The Lord had made
> the Egyptians favorably disposed toward the people,
> and they gave them what they asked for; so they
> plundered the Egyptians. (Exodus 12:33–36 NIV)

After four hundred years of bondage, the Israelites were finally free. They were not only free but also prosperous.

Continuation of Personal Story

My faith in God has always been central to who I am, even as a young child. I was now fifteen. I had been suffering from OCD for six years.

One beautiful sunny day, I walked out into the backyard and looked up toward Heaven. I thought to myself "All these thoughts about 'good luck' and 'bad luck' aren't real. God is the one in control." I chose to trust God completely, at an even deeper level than I had before. I consciously put God fully in control of my life and miraculously stopped doing the OCD behaviors!

Years later, when I saw a psychiatrist for the first time, I told him this story. He could hardly believe it. He didn't believe in God and had never heard of someone with OCD stopping doing OCD behaviors simply by putting their trust in God.

This is Philippians 4:6–7 (NIV) in action:

> Do not be anxious about anything, but in every situation, by prayer and petition, with thanksgiving, present your requests to God. And the peace of God, which transcends all understanding, will guard your hearts and your minds in Christ Jesus.

As an adult, I learned that OCD is founded on fear and anxiety. When you fully entrust your life to God, there is no need to fear. God wants to tell you today, "Don't be afraid." He has not forgotten you and the misery you are in. God's help is on the way. Keep believing!

~ OCD Revisits Later in Life ~

Unfortunately, I had to deal with OCD again when I gave birth to my first child. Not in the form of repetitive rituals this time, but in the form of intrusive thoughts.

When I told a nurse what I was experiencing, she explained that when you are a pre–teen and teenager, it is a very hormonal time, and when you've just had a baby, it is also a very hormonal time. This explained a lot. It made perfect sense. A few years later, I chose to begin taking medicine for OCD. Although I no longer suffered from repetitive rituals, I wanted to get rid of the intrusive thoughts too.

As I was approaching menopause, I was concerned that I would have another OCD episode because this is another time of life when your hormones change wildly, but thanks to God, this did not happen. I sailed through this time with ease.

Key Learnings from this Chapter

1. No matter what you are in bondage to, nothing is impossible for God to deliver you from.
2. Sometimes, things get worse before they get better. Keep holding onto God's promises.
3. No matter how things look, no matter how long you have been in bondage, keep holding onto God. Keep believing. He has not forgotten you. He will rescue you.

Prayer

Dear Lord, I have been struggling with bondage to _____ (fill in the blank). I believe that you have the power to deliver me. I ask you to deliver me and heal me in the powerful name of Jesus. Thankyou Lord. Amen.

Chapter Eleven

GOD HAS A BIGGER MIRACLE IN MIND

Trust in the Lord with all your heart and lean
not on your own understanding; in all your ways
submit to him and he will make your paths straight.
(Proverbs 3:5–6 NIV)

Have you ever hoped and prayed for something, only to feel
disappointed and disheartened when it doesn't happen? It's natural
to wonder why God allows certain things to unfold in our lives. Could
it be that he has an even bigger miracle in mind for us?

Personal Story

1. Land sale

Several years ago, we had an opportunity to sell our backyard to
a developer. We named our price, and they accepted it. We were
overjoyed. What an unexpected blessing. This would pay off a
significant portion of our mortgage, offering much–needed financial
relief. We eagerly signed the contracts and waited patiently for the
settlement period of twelve months.

Just two weeks before the settlement was due to take place, the purchasers pulled out of the sale and canceled the contract. We didn't even get to keep the 10% deposit. We were shocked and devastated that the sale had fallen through, after waiting so long. What was God doing? Why would he allow this to happen?

2.   Our Aunt Promises to Pay Off Our Mortgage.

My husband and I had a wonderful aunt who had never had a family of her own. We developed a very close bond with her over a period of twenty–five years. We visited her every week. We talked about our lives, we laughed a lot, and we ate many good meals at her house. These times were very precious to us – times we will treasure forever.

As she grew older, on several occasions, she expressed her desire to help pay off our mortgage. We were incredibly grateful for her kind offer. Eventually, she asked us to write down how much the mortgage was and what our bank details were.

Shortly after this, some of her other relatives from another state took advantage of her, forcing her to sign a Power of Attorney over to them. One of these relatives moved into her house without her permission. They took control of every aspect of her life.

We hired a barrister and tried everything we could to help her fight for her rights and her independence. Eventually, the other relatives took her to court, which she found extremely stressful. Six weeks after the second court hearing, she died. We have no doubt that the stress of these events cut our aunt's life short by years.

My husband and I were devastated to lose her. We loved her so much and she was such an integral part of our lives. Naturally, we were also disappointed that no mortgage payment was ever made.

Little did we know that God had a better plan in mind. Would it be more miraculous, for our aunt to pay off part of our mortgage, or for God to miraculously pay off the entire debt? Which option would give God greater glory?

Bible Example

The story of Lazarus illustrates a similar principle. Lazarus, a dear friend of Jesus, had fallen seriously ill.

> Now Jesus loved Martha and her sister and Lazarus. So when he heard that Lazarus was sick, he stayed where he was two more days, and then he said to his disciples, "Let us go back to Judea." John 11:5–7 (NIV)

Instead of rushing to the aid of Lazarus, Jesus waited where he was for two more days. As you keep reading the story, you can see that Jesus delayed coming on purpose. He was planning a much greater miracle than the sisters could ever have imagined.

> After he had said this, he went on to tell them, "Our friend Lazarus has fallen asleep; but I am going there to wake him up." His disciples replied, 'Lord, if he sleeps, he will get better.' Jesus had been speaking of his death, but his disciples thought he meant natural sleep. So Jesus told them plainly, 'Lazarus is dead, and for your sake I am glad I was not there, so that you may believe. But let us go to him." (John 11:11–15 NIV)

What? Jesus was glad that he was not there! How can a loving God be glad that he was not there, just when you need him the most?

By the time Jesus arrived, Lazarus had been dead for four days. The situation seemed utterly impossible.

> "Lord", Martha said to Jesus, "if you had been there, my brother would not have died. But I know that even now God will give you whatever you ask." (John 11:21–22 NIV)

Even though Martha was heartbroken because she knew that Jesus could have saved her brother, she still showed that she has faith by saying "But I know that even now, God will give you whatever you ask." (John 11:22 NIV).

> When Mary reached the place where Jesus was and saw him, she fell at his feet and said, "Lord, if you had been here, my brother would not have died." When Jesus saw her weeping, and the Jews who had come along with her also weeping, he was deeply moved in spirit and troubled. "Where have you laid him?" He asked. "Come and see, Lord," they replied. Jesus wept. (John 11:32–35 NIV)

Remember that Jesus was both fully human and fully God. When he saw the tears and the heartache of his friends, he was moved with compassion and wept with them.

> Then the Jews said, "See how he loved him!" But some of them said, "Could not He who opened the eyes of the blind man have kept this man from dying?" (John 11:36–37 NIV)

But Jesus knew what He was going to do.

> Jesus said, "Did I not tell you that if you believe, you will see the glory of God?" (John 11:40 NIV)

In other words, don't give up on God now. Hold onto your faith. God always has a greater plan. From a merely human perspective, it may look like God has failed you, but from God's perspective, it is all part of his perfect plan. It is often not until later, that we are able to look back that we see that God was there the whole time.

Have you ever heard the analogy that life is like a tapestry? We are underneath the tapestry and God is above the tapestry. From our perspective, all we can see is a big mess, with lots of knots and loose threads. But from God's perspective, it is a perfect pattern, coming together in just the right way. He is still firmly in control. Trust him, no matter what.

> Jesus called in a loud voice, "Lazarus, come out!"
> (John 11:43–44 NIV)

At Jesus' command, Lazarus came to life again and walked out of the tomb. Imagine being there and witnessing this event. Jesus knew that this was a much greater miracle than if he had merely healed him from being sick.

In Romans 8:28 (NIV) the Bible says, "We know that in all things God works for the good of those who love him."

In other words, no matter what difficulties we go through, God promises to bring good out of even the worst circumstances. Keep trusting him.

Continuation of Personal Story

About a year after our aunt passed away, God prompted us to put our old, run–down house up for sale. We put it on the market and waited to see what would happen. As I shared in Chapter 1, God helped our house sell in just six weeks, for substantially more than we thought it was worth. Three days later, God led us to the beautiful, new townhouse we live in today.

By the grace and mercy of God, we moved into our new house, completely debt–free. There was no doubt that it was God who had brought this about. God showed us that his plan was infinitely better than our plans.

Key Learnings from This Chapter

1. God doesn't always do things the way we expect him to.
2. No matter how bad our situation looks, God is still in control.
3. God feels your pain and looks upon you with compassion.
4. No matter what your circumstances look like, keep trusting God.
5. When others try to discourage your faith, don't listen to them.
6. You may not understand now, but you will understand later.
7. God takes bad situations and brings good out of them.

Prayer

Dear God, please help me to trust you when I face disappointments in my life. By faith, I know that you always have a better plan in mind. Help me to be patient and keep trusting you. In Jesus precious Name, Amen.

Part 4

COME OUT INTO
THE DEEP

Chapter Twelve

COME OUT INTO THE DEEP AND GET READY FOR A HAUL

> Put out into deep water, and let down the nets for a catch. (Luke 5:4 NIV)

The heroes of faith listed in Hebrews 11 were ordinary human beings just like you and me. Were these heroes of faith perfect? Far from it. They were sinners who failed God and needed forgiveness, just as we do. However, God still used them in remarkable ways. This gives us hope that God will work through us today, just as he did through those heroes of faith. Jesus assured us of this, saying:

> Very truly I tell you, whoever believes in me will do the works I have been doing, and they will do even greater things than these, because I am going to the Father." (John 14:12 NIV)

~ Come Out into the Deep ~

When he had finished speaking, he said to Simon, "Put out into deep water, and let down the nets for a catch." Simon answered, "Master, we've worked hard all night and haven't caught anything. But because you say so, I will let down the nets."

When they had done so, they caught such a large number of fish that their nets began to break. So, they signaled their partners in the other boat to come and help them, and they came and filled both boats so full that they began to sink.

When Simon Peter saw this, he fell at Jesus' knees and said, "Go away from me, Lord; I am a sinful man!" For he and all his companions were astonished at the catch of fish they had taken. (Luke 5:4–9 NIV)

Jesus is inviting you and me to "come out into the deep."

What does this mean in the context of faith? Many of us have ankle-deep faith. It's a safe place. We believe that God created the world and that Jesus has saved us from our sins, but we are hesitant to believe in God's miracle-working power in our lives today.

Jesus is calling each one of us to step out of the ankle-deep water where we are safe and comfortable and join him out in the deep. When we are operating out in the deep, we can no longer simply rely on our own strength and abilities, we must rely on God.

Jesus invites us to have radical, miracle-working, giant-overcoming faith, just like the heroes of faith we read about in the Bible.

Another example of coming out into the deep is the time Peter walked on the water.

Shortly before dawn Jesus went out to them, walking on the lake. When the disciples saw him walking on the lake, they were terrified. "It's a ghost," they said, and cried out in fear. But Jesus immediately said to them: "Take courage! It is I. Don't be afraid."

"Lord, if it's you," Peter replied, "tell me to come to you on the water." "Come," he said. Then Peter got down out of the boat, walked on the water and came toward Jesus. But when he saw the wind, he was afraid and, beginning to sink, cried out, "Lord, save me!" Immediately Jesus reached out his hand and caught him. "You of little faith," he said, "why did you doubt?" (Matthew 14:25–31 NIV)

As long as Peter kept his eyes on Jesus, he was able to defy the laws of gravity and walk on the water. But when he took his eyes off Jesus and looked at the storm around him, he became afraid and began to sink. What was Jesus' response? He immediately reached out and saved Peter, but he also rebuked him for his lack of faith.

~ David Triumphs Over Goliath ~

In Chapter 2, we studied the story of David and Goliath. Remember, David was just a shepherd boy. His father and brothers didn't think he was anything special.

When the prophet Samuel came to anoint the next person to be king over Israel and Samuel told Jesse to bring all his sons before him, his father didn't even bother to call David in from his sheep herding duties. Yet David was the one that God had chosen because God knew David's heart. He was devoted to God and full of faith.

We can never forget the famous speech David made when he faced the giant, Goliath. It is one of the greatest speeches of all time.

David said to the Philistine, "You come against me with sword and spear and javelin, but I come against you in the name of the Lord Almighty, the God of the armies of Israel, whom you have defied. This day the Lord will deliver you into my hands, and I'll strike you down and cut off your head. This very day I will give the carcasses of the Philistine army to the birds and the wild animals, and the whole world will know that there is a God in Israel. All those gathered here will know that it is not by sword or spear that the Lord saves; for the battle is the Lord's, and he will give all of you into our hands."

As the Philistine moved closer to attack him, David ran quickly toward the battle line to meet him. Reaching into his bag and taking out a stone, he slung it and struck the Philistine on the forehead. The stone sank into his forehead, and he fell face down on the ground. (1 Samuel 17:45–49 NIV)

In the story of David and Goliath, we see how faith in a giant God led David to overcome the seemingly impossible challenge of facing the Philistine giant.

~ All Things are Possible if You Believe ~

As we discussed in Chapter 8, Jesus often talked about the importance of faith and belief.

In Matthew 17 and Mark 9, we read about a father who brought his son to Jesus' disciples to heal him, but they were not able to. Later, when they asked Jesus why they couldn't heal him, Jesus answered "because you have so little faith." (Matthew 17:20 NIV). Jesus also expressed His frustration at their stubborn refusal to believe.

"You unbelieving and perverse generation," Jesus replied, "how long shall I stay with you? How long must I put up with you?" (Matthew 17:17 NIV)

Mark Chapter 9 relates the dialogue between Jesus and the boy's father.

Jesus asked the boy's father, "How long has he been like this?" "From childhood" he answered. "It has often thrown him into fire or water to kill him. But if you can do anything, take pity on us and help us." "If you can?" said Jesus. "Everything is possible for one who believes." Immediately the boy's father exclaimed, "I do believe; help me overcome my unbelief!" (Mark 9:21–24 NIV)

Then Jesus healed the boy.

How many of us can relate to this father? I certainly can. I do believe, and yet I also experience doubt. We have some faith, but perhaps not as great as some of the people we read about in the Bible. Perhaps we do have great faith, but only some of the time.

It is my great desire to develop this miracle–working, giant–overcoming kind of faith in God. Will you join me?

Key Learnings from this Chapter

1. The heroes of faith that we read about in the Bible were just ordinary people like you and me.
2. The faith that Jesus asks us to have does not require us to be perfect, but to have a perfect heart towards him.
3. Jesus calls us to "come out into the deep." He wants us to develop a deep and abiding faith in him. A faith where

anything is possible; where miracles can occur; where giants can be overcome and where people can be saved and healed.

4. God specializes in doing the impossible and he loves to partner with human beings to achieve his purposes.

Prayer

Dear Lord God, thank you for the faith that you have put in my heart. Help my faith to grow deeper and deeper as I walk closely with you. Thank you that you are the God of the impossible and together, we can overcome the giants in our lives. In Jesus' Name, Amen.

ABOUT THE AUTHOR

After a successful business career, Wendy Love has now dedicated her life to Christian writing and teaching. Wendy knows how to bring the Bible alive. In this book, The God of the Impossible, she reveals the greatness of God's miraculous power in the face of the impossible. She parallels powerful Bible stories with her own personal experiences including struggles with depression, anxiety, bipolar disorder, OCD, addiction, a child born with special needs, a shattered marriage, financial crises, and job loss, all of which seemed insurmountable.

Yet, Wendy's life is a testament to the extraordinary. Through her heartfelt words, she showcases the awe-inspiring ways in which God can heal wounded hearts and minds, mend broken marriages, and overcome addictions. Wendy has personally witnessed the hand of God performing miracles, including unanticipated financial blessings that could only have come by the hand of God.

Wendy's story stands as a living testament to the boundless greatness of God. Her writing radiates an authentic faith that offers readers more than hope; it offers a lifeline. In Wendy's words, you'll discover the strength to rise above life's harshest trials and the unwavering belief in the extraordinary power of God's grace to those will choose to believe.